PRENTICE HALL SERIES
IN
DECISION SCIENCES

Barry Render, Consulting Engineer
Roy E. Crummer Graduate School of Business, Rollins College

Applied Statistics

Basic Business Statistics, 4th Edition
Berenson, Levine

Statistics for Business and Economics,
2nd Edition
Berenson, Levine

*Intermediate Statistical Methods
and Applications*
Berenson, Levine, Goldstein

Elementary Business Statistics, 6th Edition
Freund, Williams, Perles

Cases in Business Statistics
Klimberg, Arnold, Berger

Business Statistics for Quality and Productivity
Levine, Ramsey, Berenson

Statistics for Management, 6th Edition
Levin, Rubin

Short Course in Business Statistics
Levin, Rubin

Applied Statistics, 4th Edition
Neter, Wasserman, Whitmore

Statistics for Business and Economics,
4th Edition
Newbold

Business Cases in Statistical Decision Making
Peters, Gray

Brief Business Statistics
Watson, Billingsley, Croft, Huntsberger

Statistics for Management and Economics,
5th Edition
Watson, Billingsley, Croft, Huntsberger

Production and Operations Management

Readings in Production and Operations
Ahmadian, Afifi, Chandler

Business Logistics Management,
3rd Edition
Ballou

Operations Strategy
Garvin

Business Forecasting, 5th Edition
Hanke, Reitsch

*Games and Exercises for Operations
Management*
Heineke, Meile

Production and Operations Management,
3rd Edition
Heizer, Render

*Cases and Readings in Production
and Operations Management*
Latona, Nathan

Managing Services, 2nd Edition
Lovelock

*Cases in Manufacturing and Service System
Management*
Mabert

Operations Management,
3rd Edition
McClain, Thomas, Mazzola

Service Operations Management
Murdick, Render, Russell

Production Planning and Inventory Control,
2nd Edition
Narasimhan, McLeavy, Billington

Principles of Operations Management
Render, Heizer

Production and Operations Management
Russell, Taylor

Plant and Service Tours in Operations Management, 4th Edition
Schmenner

Production Operations Management,
5th Edition
Schmenner

Service Operations Management
Schmenner

Topics in Just-In-Time Management
Schneiderjans

Production and Management Systems for Business (book/disk)
Sherrard, Smolin, Rodenrys

Production and Operations Management: Self-Correcting Approach, 3rd Edition
Stair, Render

Operations Strategy
Stonebraker, Leong

Principles of Inventory and Materials Management, 4th Edition
Tersine

Production Operations Management,
2nd Edition
Tersine

Management Science/Qualitative Methods

Introduction to Management Science,
5th Edition
Cook, Russell

Introductory Management Science,
4th Edition
Eppen, Gould, Schmidt

Quantitative Concepts, 2nd Edition
Eppen, Gould, Schmidt

Quantitative Decision Making for Business, 3rd Edition
Gordon, Pressman

Introduction to Management Science,
2nd Edition
Groebner, Shannon

Management Science
Mathur, Solow

Management Science, 4th Edition
Moore, Lee, Taylor

Principles of Management Science
Newbold

Quantitative Analysis for Management,
5th Edition
Render, Stair

Cases and Readings in Management Science,
2nd Edition
Render, Stair, Greenberg

Operations Research, 5th Edition
Taha

Introduction to Management Science,
5th Edition
Taylor

Principles of Operations Research,
2nd Edition
Wagner

Software

QS Version 3.0
Chang

QSB+ Version 3.0
Chang

MacQSB+
Chang

QSOM Version 3.0
Chang

Personal STORM Version 3.0
Emmons, Flowers, Khot

QM Version 3.0
Lee (AB)

POM Version 3.0
Weiss (AB)

GAMES AND EXERCISES FOR OPERATIONS MANAGEMENT

Hands-On Learning Activities for Basic Concepts and Tools

Edited by

Janelle N. Heineke

and

Larry C. Meile

Prentice Hall, Englewood Cliffs, New Jersey 07632

Library of Congress Cataloging-in-Publication Data

Games and exercises for operations management : hands-on learning
  activities for basic concepts and tools / edited by Janelle Heineke
  and Larry Meile.
      p.   cm. -- (Prentice Hall series in decision sciences)
    ISBN 0-205-16290-8
    1. Operations research--Problems, exercises, etc.   2. Production
management--Problems, exercises, etc.   I. Heineke, Janelle.
II. Meile, Larry.   III. Series.
T57.6.G35 1995   94-45578
658.4'034--dc20   CIP

Acquisitions Editor: Tom Tucker
Editorial Assistant: Diane Peirano
Cover Designer: Tom Nery
Cover Art: Steven Eppinger
Buyer: Marie McNamara

 © 1995 by Prentice-Hall, Inc.

A Simon & Schuster Company

Englewood Cliffs, New Jersey 07632

Printed in the United States of America

10 9 8 7 6 5 4 3 2 1

ISBN 0-205-16290-8

Prentice-Hall International (UK) Limited, *London*
Prentice-Hall of Australia Pty. Limited, *Sydney*
Prentice-Hall Canada Inc., *Toronto*
Prentice-Hall Hispanoamericana, S.A., *Mexico*
Prentice-Hall of India Private Limited, *New Delhi*
Prentice-Hall of Japan, Inc., *Tokyo*
Simon & Schuster Asia Pte. Ltd., *Singapore*
Editora Prentice-Hall do Brasil, Ltda., *Rio de Janeiro*

CONTENTS

PREFACE

The idea for *Games and Exercises for Operations Management* was conceived from our belief in the power of the basic tools and concepts offered by operations management and from our commitment to the idea that learning is best — and most fun — when the learner is actively engaged with the material.

We each had experience with developing exercises for use in the classroom and we were consistently impressed with how many complex and important concepts could be demonstrated in a simple game like making paper airplanes. As we studied the content of our courses, we came to the conclusion that straightforward hands-on exercises could be developed for many topics — and that our colleagues across the country had probably done just that!

We began this project by inviting those creative colleagues to share their games with us so we could share them with you. We were delighted by their submissions and hope that you will be, too.

Some games are short and can be conducted in just a portion of a class to complement a lecture or short case. Others could require a full class period or more to complete. Each exercise in this collection follows a common format that provides an introduction to the topic the game addresses, information about the number of players and their roles, a list of materials required, and detailed instructions for players. When worksheets or templates are required, they are also included. Each game is complete in itself; learners can play one or several, according to the needs of the learner and the rhythms of the course.

The Instructor's Manual supplies further information about the mechanics of each exercise, including average preparation times for instructors and students, time required in the classroom, tips for conducting the exercise, and suggestions for wrap-up and concept discussion. Each exercise is also available in Prentice Hall's Just-in-Time database, so instructors can choose those exercises that are most applicable to the concepts they cover in their particular courses.

This first volume includes games for fundamentals common to many courses (the central limit theorem and sampling, learning curve, linear programming, and simulation), product/process design, planning, and control (process design, process analysis, job shop scheduling, lot sizing, inventory management, distribution systems, MRP, and JIT), and quality management (yield, variation, quality dimensions, process capability, attribute and variables statistical process control, and experimental design). These topics are amenable to game development, and some of you may have created exercises similar to those included here. If so, we would be pleased to hear your personal "twist" or your suggestions for effective classroom use for future editions. We hope also to expand these topics in additional collections and encourage you all to send us your tried-and-true exercises — or to think about developing new ones.

Meanwhile, we hope you enjoy these games and exercises and that they contribute to the spirit of learning in your classroom.

       Janelle Heineke and Larry Meile
       Boston

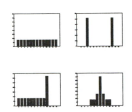

Sample Sense

Topic	Sampling from populations with different distributions
Purpose	To demonstrate the effect of the shape of the underlying distribution and the size of the sample on the shape of a distribution of sample means.
Introduction	This game is played using two decks of poker playing cards (minus jokers) shuffled together. Values are assigned to the cards so that they simulate four population distributions as shown on the worksheet pages that follow.
Materials	Two decks of standard poker playing cards per group Pencil Sampling worksheets
Players	Player #1 records sample means on chart At least one player calculates sample means
Action	Each group should thoroughly shuffle their two decks of cards together. Action takes place in two passes for each of four "populations." In the first pass, 100 samples of size two are drawn; in the second pass, 100 samples of size four are drawn. As each sample is drawn, the mean value for the sample is calculated and the recorder makes an "x" in the appropriate box on the worksheet. If the mean value is not a whole number, the value should be rounded to the nearest whole number.

Population 1: Uniform Distribution
Aces through tens are assigned their face values; jacks are worth 11, queens 12, and kings 13. In the two decks, there are eight of each card, so the frequency distribution of this population is "flat." The mean of the distribution is 7.

This exercise was created by Janelle Heineke, DBA, Assistant Professor of Operations Management at the Boston University School of Management; Boston, MA.

Population 2: Bimodal Distribution

Black cards have a value of 3; red cards have a value of 11. The mean of the distribution is 7. In the two decks, there are 52 black cards and 52 red cards.

Population 3: Skewed Distribution

Aces through tens are assigned their face values; picture cards are all assigned a value of 10. The distribution is skewed to the left (the tail of the distribution points left) and the mean of the distribution is 6.54.

Population 4: Bell-Shaped Distribution

Play for this pass is slower because each card is assigned a new value:

Card	Ace	2	3	4	5	6	7	8	9	10	J	Q	K
Value	4	5	6	6	7	7	7	7	7	8	8	9	10

The mean of this distribution is 7.

Experimentation

Try a sample of size greater than 4. What do you think should happen?

Questions for Discussion

1. How does the shape of the distribution of sample means relate to the shape of the underlying population distribution?

2. How does sample size change your ability to predict the mean of the population?

3. What happens to the spread (the standard deviation) of the sample mean distribution as sample size increases?

4. Given the shape of the distribution of sample means, how might such distributions be applied to answer real-world questions?

Worksheet #1: Uniform Distribution

Number of
Cards

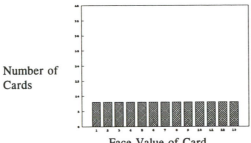

Face Value of Card

Sample Size = 2

Record an "x"
in the appropriate
column for each
trial, starting
with row #1.

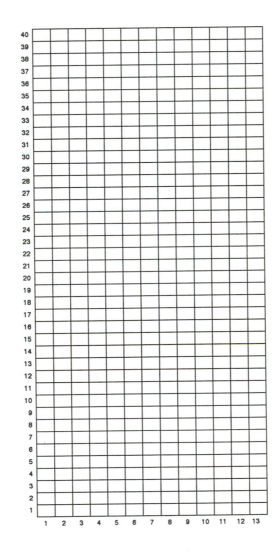

Worksheet #2: Uniform Distribution

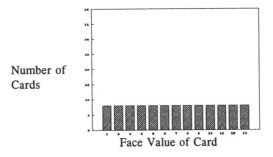

Number of
Cards

Face Value of Card

Sample Size = 4

Record an "x"
in the appropriate
column for each
trial, starting
with row #1.

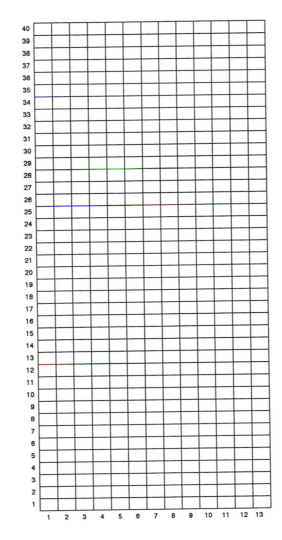

Worksheet #3: Bimodal Distribution

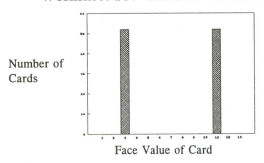

Number of
Cards

Face Value of Card

Sample Size = 2

Record an "x"
in the appropriate
column for each
trial, starting
with row #1.

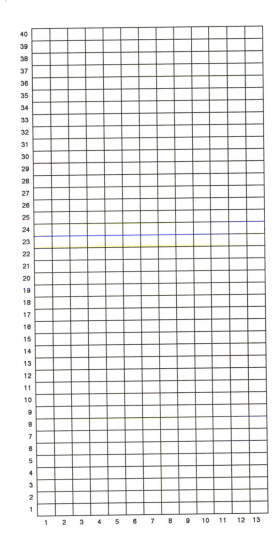

Worksheet #4: Bimodal Distribution

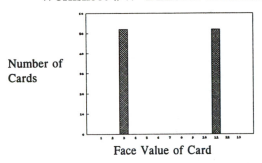

Number of
Cards

Face Value of Card

Sample Size = 4

Record an "x"
in the appropriate
column for each
trial, starting
with row #1.

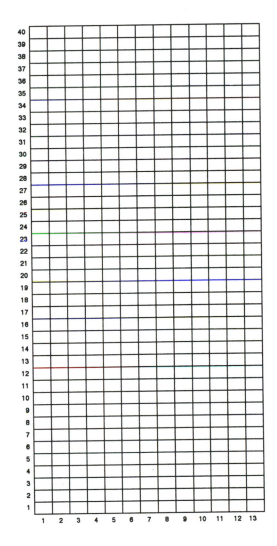

Worksheet #5: Skewed Distribution

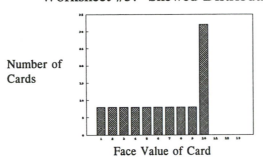

Number of
Cards

Face Value of Card

Sample Size = 2

Record an "x"
in the appropriate
column for each
trial, starting
with row #1.

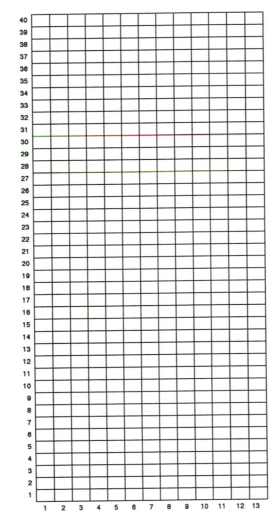

11

Worksheet #6: Skewed Distribution

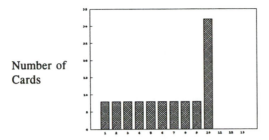

Number of
Cards

Face Value of Card

Sample Size = 4

Record an "x"
in the appropriate
column for each
trial, starting
with row #1.

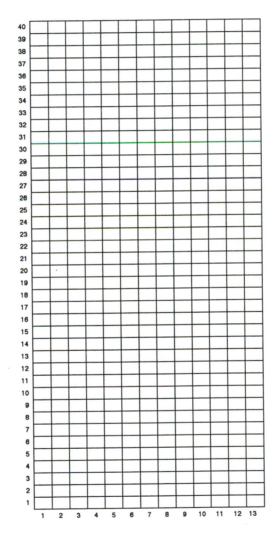

Worksheet #7: Bell-Shaped Distribution

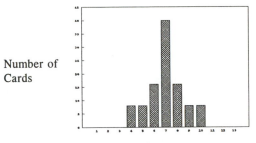

Number of
Cards

Face Value of Card

Sample Size = 2

Record an "x"
in the appropriate
column for each
trial, starting
with row #1.

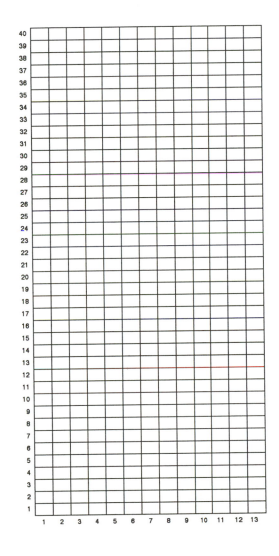

Worksheet #8: Bell-Shaped Distribution

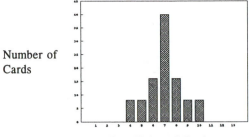

Number of Cards

Face Value of Card

Sample Size = 4

Record an "x" in the appropriate column for each trial, starting with row #1.

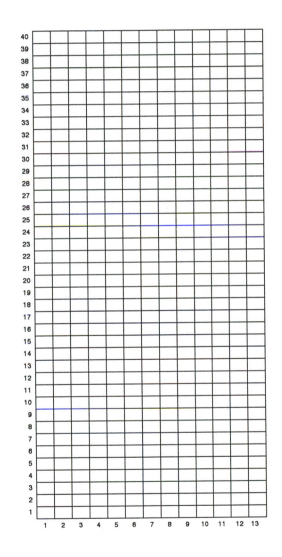

Learning Curve Cards

Topic   Learning and Experience Curves

Purpose   To demonstrate the effect of learning on the time required to perform tasks and to demonstrate the effect of designing a process for optimum performance.

Introduction   The learning curve model holds that with each doubling of cumulative production output there is a fairly consistent reduction in the direct labor hours required per unit. Each successive unit requires less time to complete than the preceding unit. This efficiency is a result of many factors, including increased worker proficiency, better use of materials, improvements in the process, and management that is more in tune to the process.

The learning curve phenomenon was first observed in the 1920s in relation to aircraft assembly processes at Wright-Patterson Air Force Base. T. P. Wright published a paper in 1936 that documented his observations. Wright found that the second plane of a given type took 80% of the labor hours required to assemble the first plane, the fourth required 80% of the labor required for the second, the eighth required 80% of the labor required for the fourth, and so on, until some logical limit is reached. The speed of learning is measured by this ratio (80%) and is called the learning rate. The lower the learning rate, the steeper the learning curve (this is one time when 60% is better than 80%!). Although much of the improvement actually comes from people figuring out how to perform their tasks more efficiently (called on-line improvement), some of the improvement stems from other sources, including new materials, new tools, or re-engineering (referred to as off-line improvements).

Learning curve theory relates direct labor hours to cumulative volume. *Learning Curve* and *Manufacturing Progress Function* are used interchangeably in the management literature. *Experience Curve*

This exercise was created by Janelle Heineke, DBA, Assistant Professor of Operations Management at Boston University, Boston, Massachusetts, and Larry Meile, Ph.D., Assistant Professor of Operations Management, Whittemore School of Business and Economics, University of New Hampshire, Durham, New Hampshire.

broadens the definition to include total costs — the costs of overhead and administration as well as direct labor hours.

This exercise demonstrates the concept of the Learning Curve in a simple production process: matching playing cards.

Materials

An ordinary deck of playing cards
A stopwatch, timer, or clock with sweep second hand
Learning Curve Recording Table and Graph

Players

Three Players:
1 Set-up Person
1 Worker
1 Timer

Action
Set-up

Sort the cards by color: red and black.

The action is performed in three passes. For each pass the task is the same: to match the face value of the red cards (held by the Worker) and the black cards, arrayed on a flat surface.

Pass 1

During Set-up the Worker should turn away from the tasks being performed. The Set-up Person shuffles the black deck thoroughly and arrays all 26 cards on a flat surface in five rows of five with the final card centered at the top of the five rows (See Figure 1). Next, the Set-up Person shuffles the red deck and hands it to the Worker, who holds it face down.

The Worker's task is to turn up one red card at a time, match the face value of the red card to one of the black cards in the array (without any attention to suit), and place the red card on top of the black card. For example, a red five is placed on a black five, a red jack is placed on a black jack, and so on. The Timer records the time it takes for the Worker to match and place all 26 cards.

The Set-up Person collects the red cards, leaving the black cards in place, and shuffles the red deck. The match-place process is repeated **three** more times. The Timer tells the Worker when to begin and records the time it takes for each repetition.

Pass 2

After Pass 1 has been completed, the Set-up person collects all the cards, keeping the reds and blacks separated, and again places the

20

black cards as shown in Figure 1 (the Worker should be turned away from the Set-up). This time, the red deck is handed to the Worker face up, so that the Worker can see the next card in the deck as he or she places a card. As in Pass 1, the Timer tells the Worker when to begin and records the time it takes to place all 26 red cards on black cards of the same face value. Perform four repetitions, collecting and shuffling only the red deck for each and leaving the black cards in their places.

Pass 3   The Set-up Person collects all the cards, keeping the reds and blacks separated, and sorts the black cards in ascending order (Ace, two, three, and so on). He or she then arrays the black cards in order as shown in Figure 2. The Set-up Person shuffles the red deck and hands the cards face up to the Worker. As in Passes 1 and 2, the Timer tells the Worker when to begin and records the time it takes to place all 26 red cards on black cards of the same face value. Perform four repetitions, collecting and shuffling only the red deck for each and leaving the black cards in their places.

Evaluation   Calculate the learning rate and plot the learning curves for each of the three passes.

Questions for Discussion

1.   What are the factors that influenced the rate of learning in this exercise?

2.   What are the managerial implications of the Learning Curve?

3.   Assume that each minute of this simulation represents a labor hour, and each labor hour costs the company $30 (salary plus benefits). Assume further that the materials cost of each unit is $20. If each repetition of the process represents the production of a unit, how is the variable cost of a unit affected by the learning rate? For each of the passes, calculate the expected variable cost of the 128th unit.

4.   What factors other than direct labor and materials need to be considered in the "cost" of the different processes in this simulation? In real production settings?

Figure 1: Set-Up for Passes 1 and 2

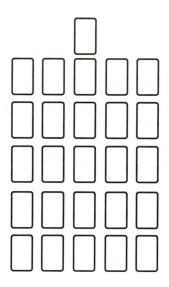

Figure 2: Set-Up for Pass 3

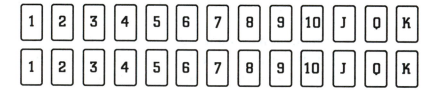

Learning Curve Recording Table

Pass	Repetition	Production Time
1	1	
	2	
	3	
	4	
2	1	
	2	
	3	
	4	
3	1	
	2	
	3	
	4	

Learning Curve Graph

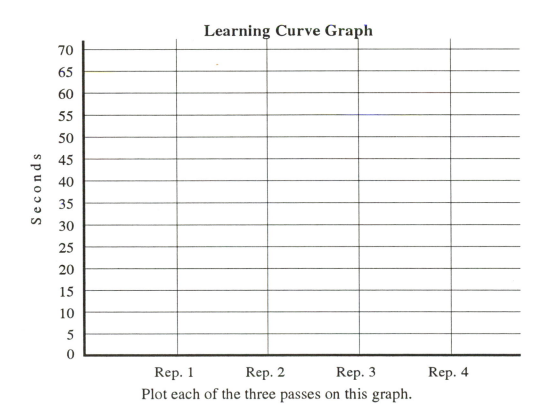

Plot each of the three passes on this graph.

23

Linear Programming using Tinkertoys[1]

Topic   Linear Programming (LP)

Purpose   This exercise explores the problem of allocating scarce resources among alternatives. A technique used to solve this frequently occurring business problem is called Linear Programming (LP). This exercise provides an intuitive starting point for understanding how to formulate and solve LP problems, and develops intuition about the fundamental economic concepts underlying the method.

Materials   88 Tinkertoy pieces shown in Required Component Set diagram (Figure 1).
Drawings and bills of material for each of three products, Robots, Turnstiles, and Front Wheel Assemblies (Figures 2, 3 and 4).
2 Recording Worksheets (Figure 5 and 6).

Players   This exercise can be done in teams of 3 to 6. A scribe should be designated to record optimal solutions. A presenter should be selected if results are to be reported to the class.

Action   For this exercise, teams are to assemble the Tinkertoy pieces into the three products. There will be two objectives. The first is to make as many of the three finished products as possible from the parts available (i.e., the number of Robots, plus the number of Turnstiles, plus the number of Front Wheel Assemblies). After this is accomplished, the second objective is to make the number of finished products that makes as much revenue as possible. The value of each toy is given in Question 2 below. The combination for the second solution may be the same as or different from the first.

A good place to start working on this problem is by identifying the parts required to make the toys and by building one of each type of toy. As building proceeds, it may be desirable to disassemble toys already made. The task is to arrive at the combination that meets the stated objective. The final solution need not include all three types of toys. In fact, the best solution may be to make only one type of toy. Use the work sheets (Figure 5 and 6) to record the solutions.

This exercise was created by Uday M. Apte, Brian T. Downs, and John R. Grout at the Edwin L. Cox School of Business, Southern Methodist University, Dallas, TX.

When the exercise is finished, please disassemble the toys completely.

**Questions for
Discussion**

1. To maximize the total number of toys, how many of each type of toy should be made?

2. Toys can be sold at the following prices: Robots, $30 each; Turnstiles, $10 each; and Front Wheel Assemblies, $20 each. In order to maximize total revenue from selling these three toys, how many of each type of toy should be made?

3. Having answered Question 2, suppose that a toy-parts trader has offered to sell your group two specific toy parts: red rods for $5 each and orange caps for $10 each. Are you interested in buying red rods? If so, how many do you want to buy? Are you interested in buying orange caps? If so, how many do you want to buy?

---

[1] Tinkertoy and Colossal Constructions are trademarks of Playskool, Inc., Pawtucket, RI 02862 USA, a subsidiary of Hasbro, Inc.

Figure 1.

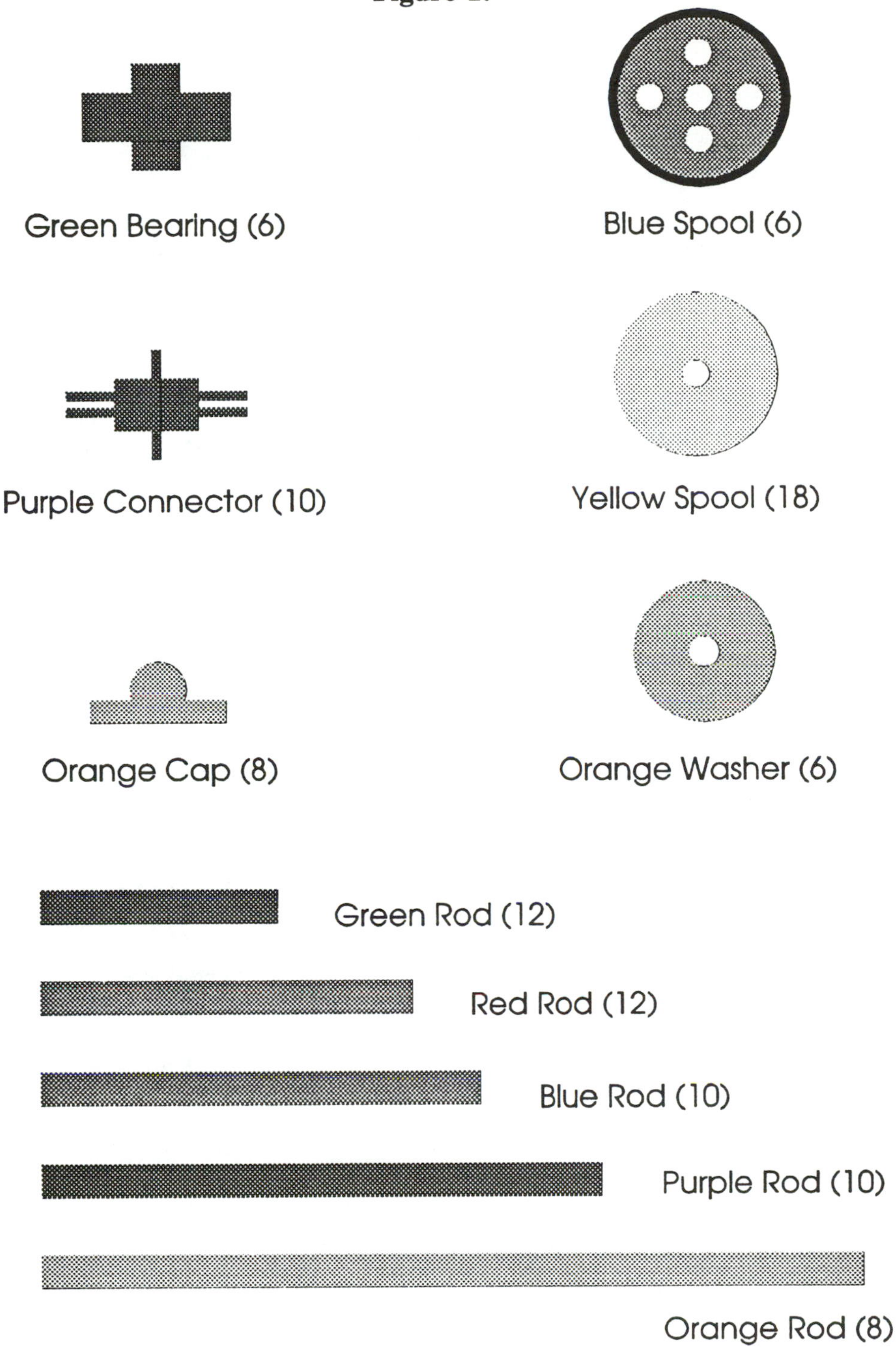

Green Bearing (6)

Blue Spool (6)

Purple Connector (10)

Yellow Spool (18)

Orange Cap (8)

Orange Washer (6)

Green Rod (12)

Red Rod (12)

Blue Rod (10)

Purple Rod (10)

Orange Rod (8)

Standard Component Set

Figure 2.

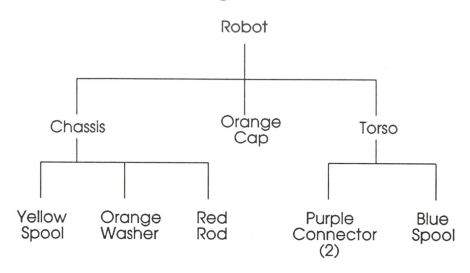

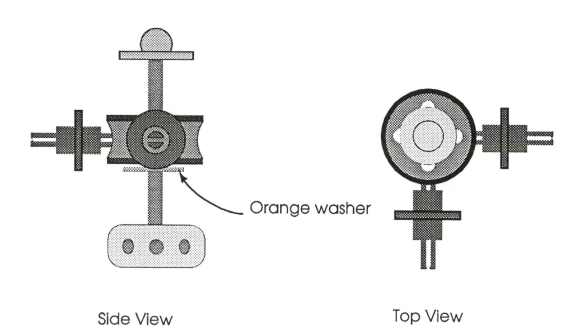

Side View

Top View

Orange washer

Robot

Figure 3.

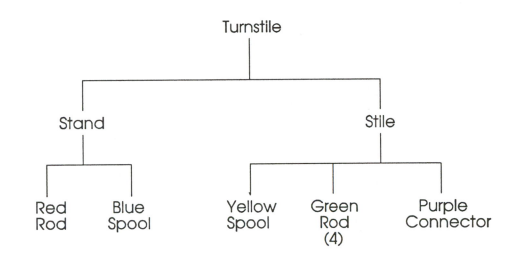

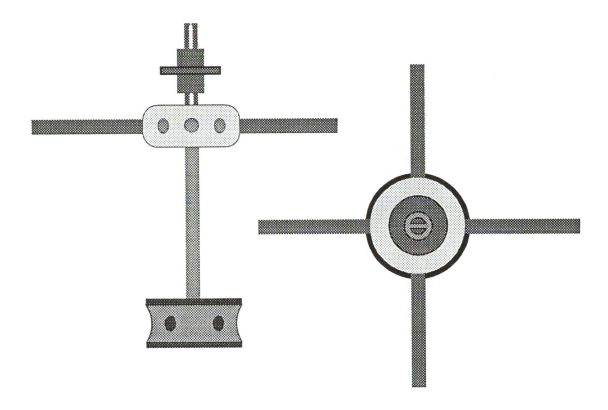

Side View   Top View

Turnstile

Figure 4.

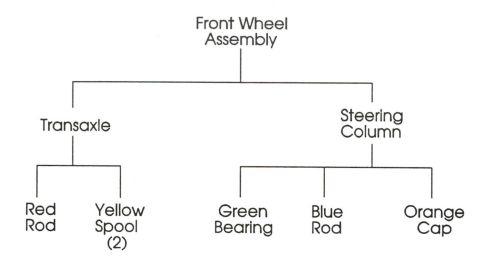

Front Wheel
Assembly

- Transaxle
  - Red Rod
  - Yellow Spool (2)
- Steering Column
  - Green Bearing
  - Blue Rod
  - Orange Cap

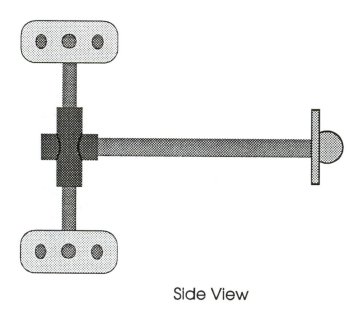

Side View

Front Wheel Assembly

Figure 5. Tinkertoy LP Exercise Worksheet #1

Maximize Total Output

Part	Number of Parts Available	Robot Prod=____		Turnstile Prod=____		Front Wheel Prod=____		Parts Left Over
		Units Req'd	Total Req'd	Units Req'd	Total Req'd	Units Req'd	Total Req'd	
Green Rods	12			4				
Red Rods	12	1		1		1		
Blue Rods	10					1		
Yellow Spools	18	1		1		2		
Blue Spools	6	1		1				
Orange Caps	8	1				1		
Orange Washers	6	1						
Green Bearings	6					1		
Purple Connectors	10	2		1				

MAXIMUM OUTPUT _____

Figure 6. Tinkertoy LP Exercise Worksheet #2

Maximize Total Revenue

Part	Number of Parts Available	Robot Prod = ___ Units Req'd	Robot Total Req'd	Turnstile Prod = ___ Units Req'd	Turnstile Total Req'd	Front Wheel Prod = ___ Units Req'd	Front Wheel Total Req'd	Parts Left Over
Green Rods	12			4				
Red Rods	12	1		1		1		
Blue Rods	10					1		
Yellow Spools	18	1		1		2		
Blue Spools	6	1		1				
Orange Caps	8	1				1		
Orange Washers	6	1						
Green Bearings	6					1		
Purple Connectors	10	2		1				
REVENUE		$30 X # Prod = ___		$10 X # Prod = ___		$20 X # Prod = ___		

MAXIMUM REVENUE = _____

Husker Dairy

Topic

Integer linear programming. Piecewise linear modeling of nonlinear curves.

Purpose

To illustrate the concepts of integer linear programming and the use of segmented constraints in an integer linear program. To present a linear programming technique for modeling a situation with decreasing marginal costs.

Introduction

Husker Dairy produces yogurt and cheese. The players are on the production management team and are responsible for determining the proper allocation of the resources of machinery (capital) and labor to produce a mix of yogurt and cheese that results in the maximum profit.

The production of a case of yogurt requires 2 machine hours and 1 labor-hour. The production of a wheel of cheese requires 2 machine hours and 2 labor-hours. Selling price for yogurt is $50 per case and for cheese is $64 per wheel.

Labor is $10/hour for the first 10 hours and $15/hour for the next 2 hours (overtime). Machine costs are $18/hour for the first 4 hours, $14/hour for the next 8 hours, and $10/hour for the remaining available 2 hours. There are only 14 machine hours available. There is a fixed cost associated with the machine operation of $8.

Materials

Machine and labor tokens.

Product containers. (These may be either paper diagrams or physical yogurt containers and cheese boxes.)

A Graphing Worksheet.

Players

Teams of two to four.

This exercise was created by Ronald T. Konecny, Ph.D., Associate Professor of Management at the College of Business and Technology, University of Nebraska at Kearney.

Action

1. Allocate the two resources (machine and labor hours) to the two products (yogurt and cheese) and determine the quantity of each to produce.

Production of the two products requires the utilization of both labor and machinery. These resources are represented by slips of paper (tokens), 14 for machine hours and 12 for labor hours. On each token is written the cost of using that particular unit of resource to produce some product.

Products are represented by yogurt containers and cheese wheels. Each unit of production has its own container. To "produce" a product, place the appropriate tokens in (on) the product to be produced.

For example, to start the process by making one case of yogurt, the top two machine hours tokens would be removed (each costing $18.00) along with one labor hour token (costing $10.00) and placed inside a yogurt container. If a wheel of cheese is to be produced next, the following two machine hour and two labor hour tokens are removed and placed inside a cheese wheel. The process of deciding the next product to make and allocating the required resources continues until the combination of products that makes the most profit is found.

Notice that the cost of machine hours decreases after the first four hours and again after the next eight hours while the cost of labor increases after eight hours. Be careful to use the appropriate tokens first. Although it would be desirable to assign the cheap machinery hours first, they don't get cheap until the initial (more expensive) hours have been used. To help prevent errors, the tokens have been numbered in the sequence they should be allocated.

2. Determine the marginal profit.

As resources are allocated to products, it is necessary to determine how much profit (or loss) has been generated by each product. Under each product write the revenue received when the product is sold, the cost of producing that product (the machine cost and the labor cost), and the resulting profit received from its production and sale.

For example, each case of yogurt sells for $50.00. The first case of yogurt produced costs $46.00, ($36.00 for two hours of machinery and $10.00 for one hour of labor). The resulting profit is $4.00.

3. Graph the results.

Every time a product is produced plot the following on the Graphing Worksheet:

> Total machine costs (don't forget the $8 fixed machine cost) against the total machine hours used up to that point.
> Total labor cost against the total labor hours used up to that point.
> Total profit against the total number of units of either yogurt or cheese produced.

Repeat steps 1, 2, and 3.

Continue to allocate the machine hours and labor hours to yogurt or cheese until one resource or the other runs out.

Experimentation   Can the profit be improved by de-allocating resources from one product and reassigning them to another? As other combinations are tried, keep the token allocation sequence in mind. Try several combinations until you feel you have reached an optimal solution.

Questions for Discussion

1. Describe the shape of the curves drawn on the three graphs.

2. As drawn, what assumptions of general linear programming are violated?

3. What variables must take on only an integer value?

4. What values that must be integer would automatically come out integer, even if they were not specified as such in the program?

5. How might non-linear relationships be represented in a linear program?

6. If segments are used, can the solution appear on more than one segment of a given function?

7. Reviewing the answers to the questions above, what must be integerized in an LP model of this situation?

Graphing Worksheet

Machine Cost versus Machine Hours

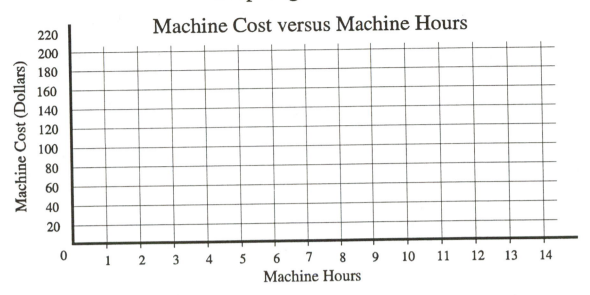

Labor Cost versus Labor Hours

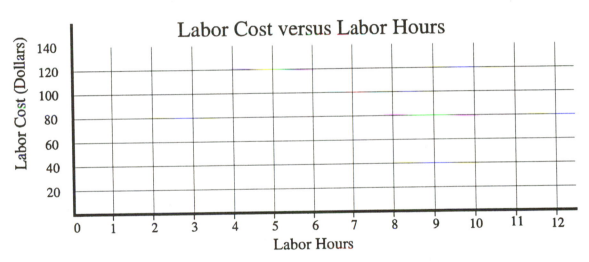

Profit versus Units of Production

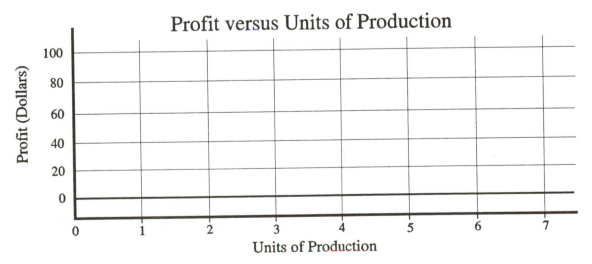

Husker Dairy Yogurt Production

Selling Price: _____

Machine Cost: _____

Labor Cost: _____

Marginal Profit: _____

Selling Price: _____

Machine Cost: _____

Labor Cost: _____

Marginal Profit: _____

Selling Price: _____

Machine Cost: _____

Labor Cost: _____

Marginal Profit: _____

Selling Price: _____

Machine Cost: _____

Labor Cost: _____

Marginal Profit: _____

Selling Price: _____

Machine Cost: _____

Labor Cost: _____

Marginal Profit: _____

Selling Price: _____

Machine Cost: _____

Labor Cost: _____

Marginal Profit: _____

Selling Price: _____

Machine Cost: _____

Labor Cost: _____

Marginal Profit: _____

Selling Price: _____

Machine Cost: _____

Labor Cost: _____

Marginal Profit: _____

41

Husker Dairy Cheese Production

Selling Price: _____
Machine Cost: _____
Labor Cost: _____
Marginal Profit: _____

Selling Price: _____
Machine Cost: _____
Labor Cost: _____
Marginal Profit: _____

Selling Price: _____
Machine Cost: _____
Labor Cost: _____
Marginal Profit: _____

Selling Price: _____
Machine Cost: _____
Labor Cost: _____
Marginal Profit: _____

Selling Price: _____
Machine Cost: _____
Labor Cost: _____
Marginal Profit: _____

Selling Price: _____
Machine Cost: _____
Labor Cost: _____
Marginal Profit: _____

Selling Price: _____
Machine Cost: _____
Labor Cost: _____
Marginal Profit: _____

Selling Price: _____
Machine Cost: _____
Labor Cost: _____
Marginal Profit: _____

Husker Dairy Production Resources

1 Machine Hour 1 @ $18/hour	1 Machine Hour 10 @ $14/hour	1 Labor Hour 1 @ $10/hour
1 Machine Hour 2 @ $18/hour	1 Machine Hour 11 @ $14/hour	1 Labor Hour 2 @ $10/hour
1 Machine Hour 3 @ $18/hour	1 Machine Hour 12 @ $14/hour	1 Labor Hour 3 @ $10/hour
1 Machine Hour 4 @ $18/hour	1 Machine Hour 13 @ $10/hour	1 Labor Hour 4 @ $10/hour
1 Machine Hour 5 @ $14/hour	1 Machine Hour 14 @ $10/hour	1 Labor Hour 5 @ $10/hour
1 Machine Hour 6 @ $14/hour	Cut these tokens apart so you can allocate them to products.	1 Labor Hour 6 @ $10/hour
1 Machine Hour 7 @ $14/hour	1 Labor Hour 12 @ $10/hour	1 Labor Hour 7 @ $10/hour
1 Machine Hour 8 @ $14/hour	1 Labor Hour 11 @ $10/hour	1 Labor Hour 8 @ $15/hour
1 Machine Hour 9 @ $14/hour	1 Labor Hour 10 @ $10/hour	1 Labor Hour 9 @ $15/hour

Door-to-Door

Topic   Simulation

Purpose   This exercise exposes students to input processes, model building, model validation, and output — four very important issues in simulation.

Introduction   Simulation is a decision-making tool that requires the development of a model of a process and testing the performance of the model under various conditions. Simulation does not find *a* solution to a problem; it either provides data which helps the modeler to see the array of possible solutions to a complex problem or tests a solution defined by the modeler. Using simulation, the decision-maker can take a *what if?* approach to understanding a problem.

Problems for which simulation is a useful technique are usually very complex. Consequently, computers are used to run many "trials" of the situation — often many thousands of trials. This exercise demonstrates the mechanics of simulation with a problem that has many potential outcomes, but which is simple enough to simulate without a computer.

Materials   A quarter, a dime, a nickel, and a penny
Simulation worksheet and a pencil or pen

Players   Two players:
One player to flip the coins
One player to record the outcome of the flips

Action   The economy is bad! You are deciding whether or not to take a part-time job selling Swapcraft parts door-to-door. The following historical sales information was collected:

1. A salesperson generally visits about 20 houses each night.
2. There is a 50% chance that someone will answer the door.

This exercise was created by Peter Arnold, Ph.D., Associate Professor of Operations Management and Ronald Klimberg, Ph.D., Assistant Professor of Operations Management, Boston University, Boston, Massachusetts.

3. If a man answers the door, there is a 25% chance that he will buy two parts and a 25% chance that he will purchase one part.
4. If a woman answers the door, there is a 25% chance that she will buy one part.
5. Swapcraft's compensation to the salesperson is $5 per part.

To simulate the result of each sales call you will need four coins; a quarter, a dime, a nickel, and a penny.

- The quarter represents the random variable of someone answering the door.

- The dime determines whether a male or female answers the door.

- The combination of the nickel and penny determines the success of the sales call.

The following table provides the translation of the various combinations of coin flips and the resulting sales.

Quarter	Dime	Nickel	Penny	Outcome
HEADS				No one home!
TAILS	HEADS			Woman answers
		HEADS	HEADS	1 part sold
		All others		0 parts sold
	TAILS			Man answers
		HEADS	HEADS	2 parts sold
		TAILS	TAILS	1 part sold
		All others		0 parts sold

Simulate one night's work (twenty calls), recording the number of coins flipped and parts sold on the simulation worksheet. How did you do? Should you take the job?

Questions for Discussion

1. What additional piece of information is critical for making your decision about taking the Swapcraft job?

2. How confident are you about your decision to take the job after simulating one night's work? How many nights would you want to simulate before you made your decision?

3. How could you test for changing market conditions? How important would this be for making your decision?

Door-To-Door Simulation Worksheet

Call Number	Coins Flipped	Parts Sold
1		
2		
3		
4		
5		
6		
7		
8		
9		
10		
11		
12		
13		
14		
15		
16		
17		
18		
19		
20		
21		
22		
23		
24		
25		
26		
27		
28		
29		
30		

Olympic Hats

Topic   Evaluating an Investment Decision Using Simulation

Investment decisions often involve factors about which we are uncertain. Modeling can improve our understanding of the potential outcomes of different decisions. One way of modeling situations that have multiple factors is through the technique of computer simulation.

Purpose   This exercise demonstrates how a business decision can be modeled and how the Monte Carlo method is used to generate input values for the model according to a predefined distribution.

Introduction   A group of entrepreneurial students is evaluating the production of hats for the Olympic Games. The required initial investment including a one-year licensing agreement with the International Olympic Committee is $350,000. They have established that the variable cost per hat will be $5.00. It is not known with certainty how many hats will be sold or what unit price the Olympic Committee will finally agree upon, but these two variables are independent and their distributions have been estimated as shown in Figure 1.

Units Sold (Thousands)	Probability
200	0.40
300	0.30
400	0.30

Unit Price	Probability
$6.00	0.20
$7.00	0.60
$8.00	0.20

Figure 1. Volume and Price Distributions

The demand for these hats would be short-lived so the time value of money may be disregarded.

This exercise was created by Ismael G. Dambolena, Professor of Management Science at Babson College, Wellesley, Massachusetts and Larry Meile, Assistant Professor of Decision Sciences at the Whittemore School of Business and Economics, University of New Hampshire, Durham, NH.

If you were the decision maker, what information would you like to have in order to make a decision? Think about this before you go on.

Modeling the Situation

You have probably concluded, as most investors would, that what you would like to know is how profitable this investment will be. If you knew exactly how many hats were to be sold and what price you would be able to get for each hat you could calculate total revenue. You would produce as many units as you could sell and, since you know the per unit cost, you can calculate the total variable cost. Adding this to the initial investment cost, you could calculate total cost. Total revenue minus total cost is the resulting profit. This can be expressed using the equation:

$$\text{Profit} = \text{Total Revenue} - \text{Total Cost}$$

Substituting the expressions that represent total revenue and total cost we obtain a more detailed equation:

$$\text{Profit} = \text{Units (Unit Price)} - (\text{Investment} + \text{Units (Unit cost)})$$

The profit resulting from the sale of Olympic hats depends on two random variables (Sales and Price) and, as a consequence, is itself a random variable. Therefore, you cannot know the profit with certainty ahead of time but you can estimate the expected profit and its variance.

The *most* you can learn about any random variable is its frequency distribution. But, once you know the distribution, you can compute its expected value, its variance, its standard deviation, its range, its percentiles, and so on. By knowing its distribution, you know as much about a random variable as you possibly can know before seeing it take on an actual value.

Figure 1 gives estimates of the distribution for units sold and the distribution of unit price. Each combination of these two random variables gives a different result when used in the profit equation shown above. Also, each combination has a different probability of occurring, and therefore has a different degree of influence on the expected outcome.

Keeping this in mind, how can you estimate the distribution of the profit for this investment?

Probability Trees

A probability tree can be used to estimate the distribution of the profit for the investment. The tree in Figure 2 has nine paths from the single root node on the left to the tips of the nine end branches on the right. Each path represents a different possible combination of one sales volume and one unit price, and therefore exactly one of these paths will "happen" if the Olympic hat is produced. Each path has a profit associated with it. For example, values represented by the bottom path that leads to the end branch on the bottom right are a sales volume of 400,000 units and a unit price of $8.00. Under all conditions there is the fixed $350,000 investment cost and a unit cost of $5.00. Using the profit equation from the second page, we get

Profit = Total Revenue   — Total Cost
        = 400,000 hats ($8/hat) — ($350,000+400,000 hats ($5/hat))
        = $3,200,000   — $2,350,000
        = $850,000

The profits of the different paths are listed in Figure 2 under the heading "Profit" on the branches to the right.

Each path also has a probability of occurring. Since the two variables in each path are statistically independent, the probability of a path occurring is the product of the two branch probabilities in that path. (Branch probabilities are shown on the tree under all branches.) The probability that the bottom path occurs, for instance, is

P(units sold = 400,000) × P(unit price = $8.00)
= 0.30 × 0.20
= 0.06

The probabilities of the different paths are listed in Figure 2 next to their profits. If the two variables were statistically dependent, we would need information on their conditional probabilities but the overall modeling method would still be the same.

Fixed cost = $350,000

Variable cost = $5/unit

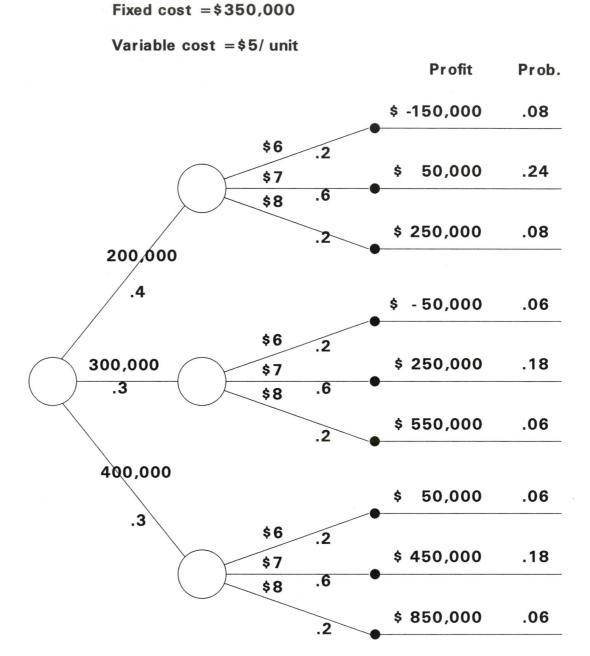

Figure 2. Probability Tree

In order to obtain the estimated distribution of the profitability for this investment we now sort the path profits in ascending order along with their corresponding probabilities. When there are several paths with the same profit we **add** the probabilities of these paths. The resulting distribution is shown below.

Profit (Thousands of dollars)	Probability
-150	0.08
-50	0.06
50	0.30
250	0.26
450	0.18
550	0.06
850	0.06

Figure 3. The Resulting Calculated Distribution

From this distribution we learn that this investment in Olympic hat production may produce profits of up to $850,000 but also losses of up to $150,000. There is a 14% chance of losing some money. The expected profit can be computed from the distribution (it is $230,000). The standard deviation and variance of profits (both measures of the risk of the investment) can also be computed now that we know the distribution.

A graph of this distribution shows that it is quite different from other common distributions (such as normal, Poisson, uniform, etc.). See Figure 4. This implies that the mathematics that are appropriately applied to these special distributions would not apply to this case. Therefore, analyzing this problem by assuming it can be reasonably approximated by a standard situation would yield erroneous results. Methods for dealing with unusual distributions must be used. The probability tree analysis we just did is one of these methods. The simulation technique that follows is another.

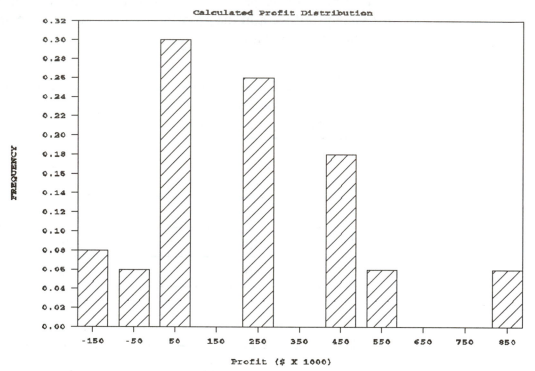

Figure 4

Simulation

The procedure we just followed, though useful from a conceptual standpoint, was rather time consuming, despite the fact that only two variables were involved and each variable had only three possible values. In a real investment decision many variables come into play: total market size, market growth rate, market share, selling price, total investment required, useful life of the facilities, residual value of facilities, and operating costs, among others. Moreover, most of these variables have a very wide range of possible values. Modeling of such a complex problem using a probability tree would not be practicable.

For a large and complex problem, computer simulation is a much better modeling approach. Simulation is a procedure which uses a mathematical model of the decision and feeds values to the model to get results. In this case, the mathematical model is the profit equation we used earlier. Instead of calculating each possible outcome and the probability of that outcome as we did using the probability tree, values for Price and Units Sold are randomly selected and fed into the model. This process is done many times and the resulting distribution of profits is recorded.

The key question here is how to get the values for the random variables (Price and Units Sold) fed into the model in proportion to their likelihood of occurring. How would you do this simulation "by hand" using the two dials shown in Figure 5, one for randomly generating sales volumes and the other one for randomly generating unit prices?

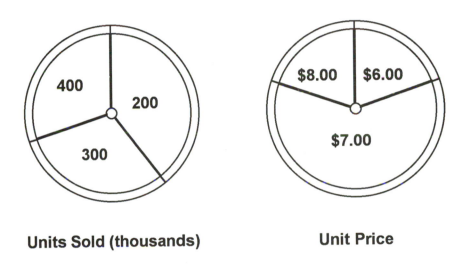

Units Sold (thousands)   **Unit Price**

Figure 5

Materials   Two large cardboard dials similar to those in Figure 5. Each dial has an arm, like on a clock, that can be rotated. The rims of the dials are divided into ten equal sectors numbered zero through nine.

A random number generator capable of producing single digits 0-9. (This can be accomplished with a random number table, a deck of cards; Ace through 10; — J, Q and K removed, or with a computer.)

Players   Seven Players:

Players #1 and #2 generate random digits, one for each dial.

Players #3 and #4 are each assigned to a dial. When a random digit is generated, the arm of the sales volume dial is moved accordingly and held there (to obtain a random sales volume). In a similar way a unit price is generated randomly.

Player #5 records the sales volume and unit price, then computes and records the resulting profit. Player #6 checks the computations made by Player #5.

Player #7 graphs the results.

Action   Players #1 and #2 generate random single digits. Players #3 and #4 use the digits to select among the ten sectors on the rim and rotate the arm so that it will point to the selected sector. The resulting simulated value appears under the arm. Player #5 records the simulated values of the sales volume and price, then calculates and records the resulting profit in the simulation table provided. Player #6 assists Player #5.

Player #7 graphs the results of each trial on the histogram worksheet provided.

Repeat the action at least 100 times. Observe how the histogram develops.

**Questions
for Discusion**

1. How does the simulation histogram compare to the distribution that was created using the probability tree?

2. How could you make the simulation histogram more closely match the distribution created using a probability tree?

3. How could you use a spreadsheet to perform this simulation?

Simulation Worksheet

Trial	Volume	Price	Profit
1			
2			
3			
4			
5			
6			
7			
8			
9			
10			
11			
12			
13			
14			
15			
16			
17			
18			
19			
20			
21			
22			
23			
24			
25			
26			
27			
28			
29			
30			
31			
32			
33			
34			
35			
36			
37			
38			
39			
40			
41			
42			
43			
44			
45			
46			
47			
48			
49			
50			

Trial	Volume	Price	Profit
51			
52			
53			
54			
55			
56			
57			
58			
59			
60			
61			
62			
63			
64			
65			
66			
67			
68			
69			
70			
71			
72			
73			
74			
75			
76			
77			
78			
79			
80			
81			
82			
83			
84			
85			
86			
87			
88			
89			
90			
91			
92			
93			
94			
95			
96			
97			
98			
99			
100			

Histogram Worksheet

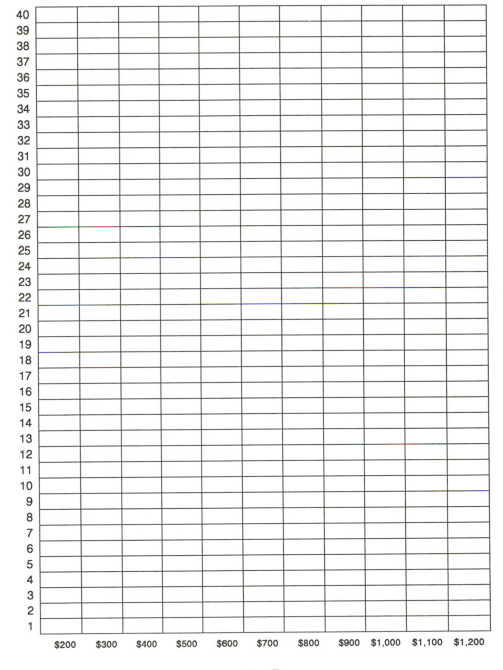

Record an "x" in the appropriate column for each trial, starting with row #1.

Profit

The Simkin Inventory Decision

Topic   Monte Carlo simulation of quantity/reorder inventory policy

Purpose   To introduce the topic of Monte Carlo simulation of inventory with variability of both product demand and vendor lead time.

Introduction   Among the many products stocked by the Simkin Hardware Store is the ACE Model 89 Electric Drill. Sales of the drill have been rather low and variable over the last year. Even though the sales are not high, the quality of the drill is excellent and the per unit profits are good. Simkin wants to offer a complete product line, so continued stocking of the ACE "89" is desirable. The demand profile for the ACE Drill is shown below in **Table 1**.

Table 1: Demand Profile for the ACE Drill

Daily Demand	Frequency	Probability	Cumulative Probability	Random Numbers
0	10	0.05	0.05	00 to 04
1	20	0.10	0.15	05 to 14
2	40	0.20	0.35	15 to 34
3	80	0.40	0.75	35 to 74
4	30	0.15	0.90	75 to 89
5	20	0.10	1.00	90 to 99
TOTALS	200	1.00		

This exercise was created by William R. Benoit, Ph.D., Associate Professor of Operations Management, Plymouth State College, Plymouth, New Hampshire.

Lead times for deliveries have also exhibited variance. The lead time profile for the drill is shown below in **Table 2.**

Table 2: Lead Time Profile for ACE Drill

Lead Time	Frequency	Probability	Cumulative Probability	Random Numbers
1	8			
2	20			
3	12			
Totals	40			

The store owner, Art Simkin, is troubled by the rising number of customer complaints that the store is out of drills. Because customers usually have an urgent need for products when they come into the store, in the event of a stock-out they go across the street to purchase their desired product from Simkin's strongest competitor. Because drills are durable goods, the loss due to lost sales is a permanent loss.

Lately, Art has ordered 10 drills (Q) at a time and reordered when 5 drills (R) remain in stock. Art knows his holding costs are low because his average inventory is low. But he is very concerned about the high opportunity cost of the stock-outs as well as the rising customer complaints. Another concern is the increased cost of ordering when the ordering quantity is small.

Cost factors for the drill are shown below:

Cost to place each **order**	**$10.00**
Cost to **hold** one drill each day	**0.50**
Opportunity cost of one **lost sale**	**8.00**

Materials   Inventory Simulation Worksheet
Table of Pseudo-Random Numbers

Players   Any number may participate; most effective in small groups.

Action

As a consultant to the Simkin Hardware Store, you have decided to conduct a Monte Carlo Simulation of ordering policies for the ACE Model 89 Electric Drill. The Senior Consultant (your instructor) has asked you to set up the simulation and will assign the order quantity (Q) and the reorder point (R) to be simulated.

First, the Senior Consultant will take you through a 10-day simulation, step-by-step. You will be trained on the completed 10-day simulation below which models Art's current policy of $Q = 10$ and $R = 5$. This will show you how to bring the economic factors into the simulation model as well as teaching you the basic Monte Carlo simulation method.

After your initial session with the Senior Consultant, develop a 10-day simulation of the ordering policy (Q and R combination) assigned, and determine the average daily cost. In addition to assigning a Q and R combination, the instructor will assign each participant or group a column or row of random numbers for both demand and lead times. Remember, you must use the random numbers in the specific order recorded in the table, and you must not determine both demand and lead time from the same stream of random numbers. (Doing so "de-randomizes" the numbers and creates destructive variance and biased results.)

Prepare to report your results to the Senior Consultant and to discuss the simulation you conducted.

Questions for
Discussion

1. Was your Q and R combination a "good" inventory policy?

2. You simulated 10 days of operation with the ACE Drill. Was this sample size of 10 sufficient to make a decision on the optimum Q and R?

4. What is the significance of the average random number?

4. How could the other row averages be used by the inventory manager?

5. Is it possible Art has been too aggressive in reducing inventory in an attempt to lower holding costs?

Table of Pseudo-Random Numbers

ROW	COLUMN									
	1	2	3	4	5	6	7	8	9	10
1	95	67	24	76	64	02	53	16	55	54
2	92	16	03	19	69	02	90	23	91	71
3	80	55	94	60	41	89	22	19	75	12
4	89	41	12	46	14	75	93	14	07	03
5	48	65	09	06	37	74	83	17	69	10
6	96	74	93	60	85	25	61	03	68	89
7	62	03	95	70	52	16	43	41	56	42
8	88	90	44	29	99	20	42	63	82	19
9	03	07	09	77	09	82	75	56	56	40
10	97	44	71	01	46	37	00	53	10	79
11	78	21	96	80	16	59	18	13	74	30
12	76	67	06	89	59	87	27	07	71	54
13	92	17	78	67	30	68	56	71	06	46
14	39	85	72	91	11	23	36	61	66	68
15	48	24	46	57	55	60	84	75	36	35
16	49	68	95	21	01	71	22	43	29	49
17	25	76	77	74	26	21	09	38	13	75
18	71	91	14	42	11	60	82	20	68	78
19	29	50	44	57	21	72	03	14	92	44
20	25	89	45	51	74	78	49	93	14	83

Notes:

1. Row #1 and first two numbers of Row #2 taken from sample simulation in original Simkin case.

2. Balance of table generated using *Lotus 1-2-3* by the author.

SAMPLE INVENTORY SIMULATION WORKSHEET

Order Quantity (Q) _____   Reorder Point (R) _____

Simulation Parameters	DAY 1	2	3	4	5	6	7	8	9	10	Row Total	Row Average
Units Received	0	0	0	0	10	0	0	0	10	0	20	2.0
Beginning Inventory	10	5	2	0	10	7	7	4	12	9	66	6.0
Random Number	95	67	24	76	64	02	53	16	55	54	506	50.6
Demand	5	3	2	4	3	0	3	2	3	3	28	2.8
Ending Inventory	5	2	0	0	7	7	4	2	9	6	42	4.2
Lost Sales	0	0	0	4	0	0	0	0	0	0	4	0.4
Place an Order?	yes	no	no	no	no	no	yes	no	no	no	2	0.2
Random Number	92	-	-	-	-	-	16	-	-	-	108	54.0
Lead Time (days)	3	-	-	-	-	-	1	-	-	-	4	2.0
Ordering Cost ($)	10	0	0	0	0	0	10	0	0	0	20	$2.00
Carrying Cost ($)	2.5	1	0	0	3.5	3.5	2	1	4.5	3	21	$2.10
Stockout Cost ($)	0	0	0	32	0	0	0	0	0	0	32	$3.20
Total Daily Cost	12.5	1	0	32	3.5	3.5	12	1	4.5	3	$73	$7.30

TOTAL DAILY COST ($)   =   **$73.00** for a 10 day simulation

AVERAGE DAILY COST ($)   =   **$73.00** for a 10 day simulation

70

INVENTORY SIMULATION WORKSHEET

The Simkin Inventory Decision

Order Quantity (Q) _____   Reorder Point (R) _____

Simulation Parameters	DAY 1	2	3	4	5	6	7	8	9	10	Row Total	Row Average
Units Received												
Beginning Inventory												
Random Number												
Demand												
Ending Inventory												
Lost Sales												
Place an Order?												
Random Number												
Lead Time (days)												
Ordering Cost ($)												
Carrying Cost ($)												
Stockout Cost ($)												
Total Daily Cost												

TOTAL DAILY COST ($)   =   _____   for a 10 day simulation

AVERAGE DAILY COST ($)   =   _____   for a 10 day simulation

The Ball Game

Topic   Process Analysis

Purpose   The objective of this exercise is to demonstrate the effect of change on processes within organizations.

Materials   Tennis Balls

Players   Two teams of six ball passers
One Timer for each team
Observers

Action   The team of ball passers should take a tennis ball and develop a pattern for passing the ball. The only requirement is that every person in the group must handle the ball before the pattern repeats itself. Once the pattern is established, pass the ball for several rounds so the timer can gather data.

        The timer is responsible for timing an iteration of passing the ball from player to player and recording that time.

        Observers should watch the groups and be prepared to comment on the way they went about their task.

Experimentation Instructor will introduce variation to the process.

Questions for Discussion

1. What did class members observe?

2. What did the exercise feel like to group members?

3. What did this exercise demonstrate about change that you might apply to your own organization?

4. How do the efficiency measures compare across the two groups? How was the performance measure (timing) affected by changes to the process?

This exercise was created by Susan West Engelkemeyer, Ph.D., Director of Quality and Assistant Professor of Management, Babson College, Wellesley, MA.

Cellulose Aircraft, Inc.

Topic   Production Processes

Purpose   This exercise illustrates the contrast between craft production and mass production and introduces students to the fundamental concepts of work simplification and line balancing.

Introduction   In this production simulation, players produce paper aircraft following nine steps:

Materials   Aircraft preforms (about 200)
(per line)   Cardboard carton (at least 1 x 2 feet in size)
                     Clock or timer
                     Role of masking tape
                     Table arranged so that workers can stand at side-by-side workstations
                     Cellulose Aircraft Worksheet

Players   Ten Players:
                     8 Production Workers
                     1 Test Pilot
                     1 Timer/Recorder

Action
Set-up   Define a launching line from which planes will be test launched. Mark the line with masking tape. Six to eight feet from the launching line place an open cardboard carton.

                     Aircraft are produced following these nine steps:

                     1. Write an aircraft identification number in the serial number box on Side 2 of the preform (aircraft pattern); turn the preform so that Side 1 is facing up.

                     2. Fold #1: The first right nose sweep

                     3. Fold #2: The first left nose sweep

This exercise was created by William R. Benoit, Ph.D., Associate Professor of Management, and Duncan C. McDougall, Associate Professor of Operations Management, Plymouth State College, Plymouth, New Hampshire.

4. Fold #3: Fold sheet of paper in half lengthwise

5. Fold #4: Second right nose sweep

6. Fold #5: Second left nose sweep

7. Fold #6: Third (last) right nose sweep

8. Fold #7: Third (last) left nose sweep

9. Acceptance Test Flight: Stand behind the launching line and fly the aircraft into the box. If the test pilot misses, he or she must retrieve the aircraft, adjust the trim tabs if necessary, and try again. Each aircraft must be successfully tested (flown into the box) in order of production before the next aircraft can be tested. The serial numbers help to control the flight testing sequence.

Practice

Each worker should produce an aircraft and practice flying it twice before the start of the simulation. The trim tabs may need to be curved upward slightly to control the flight of the aircraft.

**Pass 1
Craft Production**

Each worker will produce and test his or her own aircraft.
The Timer stops production after exactly five minutes and records the number of planes in the box and computes the average output per worker.

What did you observe about the process? Did all aircraft take the same amount of time to produce and test? If not, to what can you attribute the variation?

**Pass 2
Line Flow 1**

The supply of preforms is relocated to the head of the line and each worker performs one step in the process. The Timer again stops production after exactly five minutes and records the results.

How did the line flow process differ from the craft production process? What were the implications for the workers? What were the implications for the process as a whole?

Pass 3
Revised Line Flow   Take five minutes to analyze the production process and make recommendations for improvement. Recommendations must fall within the following guidelines: 1) No additional workers may be "hired" and all workers must be assigned a task.

Reset the work stations to accommodate the agreed-upon revisions and restart production. The Timer again stops production after exactly five minutes and records results.

Evaluate the results of the changes to the process.

Cellulose Aircraft Worksheet

Production Method	Number of Workers	Number of Acceptable Aircraft	Average Output Per Worker
Craft Production			
Line Flow 1			
Revised Line Flow			

Cellulose Aircraft

Fold #2

Fold #1

Fold #7

Fold #6

Fold #3

SIDE 1

Left Trim Tab

Right Trim Tab

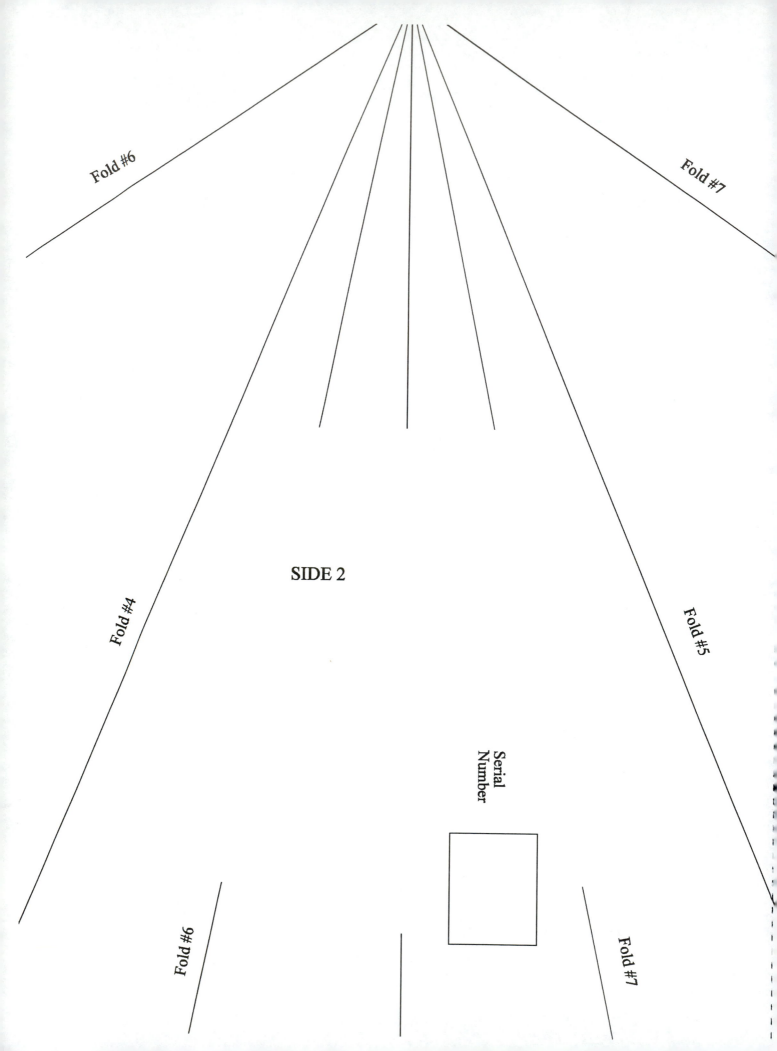

Fold #6

Fold #7

SIDE 2

Fold #4

Fold #5

Serial
Number

Fold #6

Fold #7

Paper Puppets

Topic	Assembly Line Balancing
Purpose	To demonstrate the challenges of managing a line production system, including issues of balance and workforce management.
Materials	20 pieces of paper One ruler Colored markers Puppet template (see Figure 1) Puppet Production Table
Players	11 Players: 3 Assembly Workers 3 Task Timers 3 Throughput Timers 1 Conformance Inspector 1 Supervisor
Action	There are three sets of tasks for the production of puppets. Each Assembly Worker performs the task set at his or her own pace.

Assembly Workers

Task 1. Fold bottom of paper to right side to define a square. Fold top of paper down, creasing fold sharply, and remove excess. Fold second diagonal of square.

Task 2. Fold each corner of square inward toward center. Flip over.

Task 3. Fold each corner of square inward to center. Flip square over. Draw eyes and tongue as shown in Figure 1.

This exercise was created by Janelle Heineke, DBA, Assistant Professor of Operations Management, Boston University, Boston, Massachusetts and Larry Meile, Ph.D., Assistant Professor of Operations Management, Whittemore School of Business and Economics, University of New Hampshire, Durham, New Hampshire.

Figure 1: Puppet Tasks

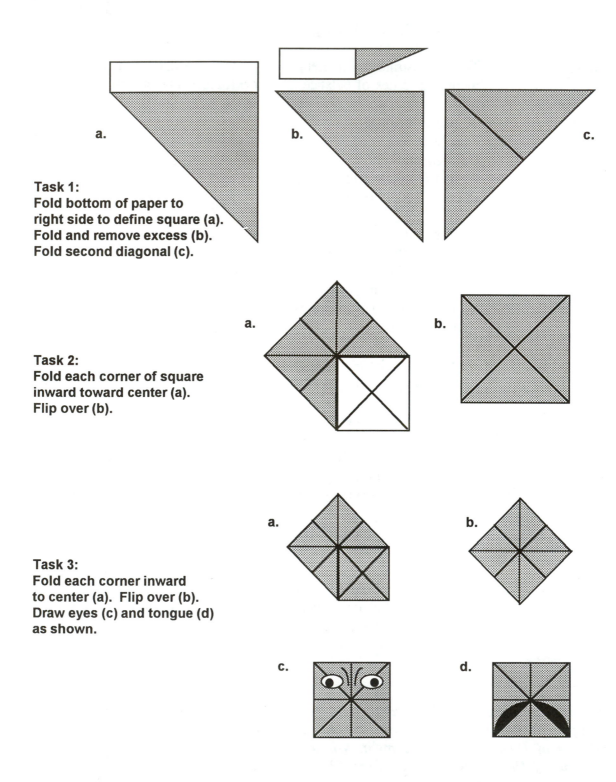

Task 1:
Fold bottom of paper to
right side to define square (a).
Fold and remove excess (b).
Fold second diagonal (c).

Task 2:
Fold each corner of square
inward toward center (a).
Flip over (b).

Task 3:
Fold each corner inward
to center (a). Flip over (b).
Draw eyes (c) and tongue (d)
as shown.

Each worker is timed by a Task Timer. The Task Timer for each task should record task time for the production of each unit, calculate mean task time, and write maximum task time, minimum task time, and mean task time on the Production Table.

The total throughput time for each unit is monitored by the Throughput Timers. For each unit, Throughput Times should record the time at which work is started at Task 1 and the time the unit is completed at Task 3.

The Conformance Inspector measures the folds on completed units. He or she should reject any units that have folds that are more than 1/8 inch out of alignment. Rejected units should be returned to the Assembly Worker at Task 1. The unit should be passed along the line with each worker checking his or her own work and reworking as necessary.

The Supervisor will define his or her own role.

Stop the process after 10 units have been accepted by the Conformance Inspector.

Experimentation   Discuss alternatives for improving the efficiency of the system. Implement suggestions and re-run the exercise for the production of ten more unit.s

Questions for Discussion

1. What did you observe about:

   a. Balance of the line?
   b. Idle time?
   c. Throughput time?
   d. How the supervisor defined his or her role?
   e. How task times changes as the simulation continued?
   f. How workers appear to react to their jobs?

2. What were the effects of process improvements?

3. Can a perfectly balanced line be achieved? If so, how?

Puppet Production Table

Unit #	Throughput Timers			Task Timers		
	Start Time	Complete Time	Through put Time	Task 1	Task 2	Task 3
1						
2						
3						
4						
5						
6						
7						
8						
9						
10						
Mean	XXX	XXX				
11						
12						
13						
14						
15						
16						
17						
18						
19						
20						
Mean	XXX	XXX				

Shell Game

Topic
Job Shop Scheduling

Purpose
The purpose of this exercise is to demonstrate the production challenges of a job shop environment.

In this demonstration, four workcenters produce 24 jobs. Each job requires the performance of a single operation at each workcenter. Process times and routes vary across the 24 jobs.

The product is a "four-layered box." The box begins production as a white card (See Figure 1) which has twelve shells that have been divided into four layers. Each layer is to be colored a different color. The finished product is the card after it has been colored.

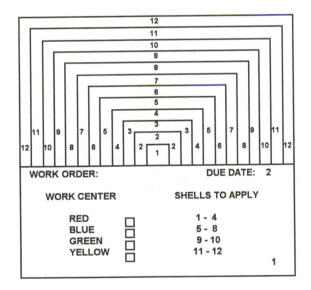 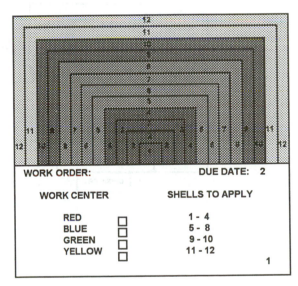

Figure 1

This exercise was created by James Ward and Leroy B. Schwarz, Krannert Graduate School of Management, Purdue University.

There are four workcenters: red, blue, green, and yellow. Each has a single operator equipped with a felt marker or crayon. There are 24 jobs, each requiring one operation at each of the four workcenters. Each job has a different route printed on card below the shells. Each workcenter has an "in-area," a dispatcher, and an "out-area." (See a typical layout in Figure 2.) The dispatcher oversees the queue of jobs in the in-area and sequences the jobs through the workcenter.

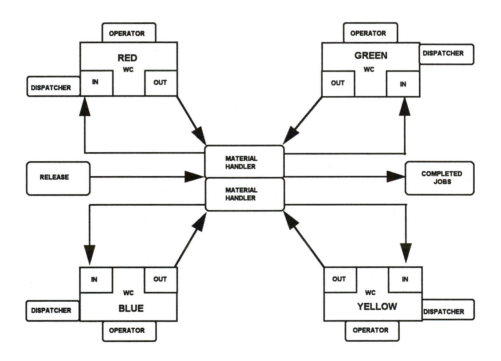

Figure 2

Materials

Blank production cards: Masters of the 24 blank cards are provided at the end of the exercise. They should be copied and cut apart.

Red, blue, green, and yellow markers

Stopwatch or watch with a sweep second hand

Players

Four operators: red, blue, green, yellow
One recorder
Four dispatchers: red, blue, green, yellow
Two material handlers

Action

Illustration

To illustrate the process, consider the job shown in Figure 1. Its first operation is at the red workcenter because "red" is at the top of the route as shown on the blank card. The blank card is initially released into the red in-area (along with several other jobs). The dispatcher at the red workcenter chooses which job from the queue to give the operator, using any dispatching rule he or she desires. When it comes time to process this job, the operator colors shells 1 through 4 red, marks the box next to "red" to indicate a completed operation, and places the job in the out-area. A material handler, noting the job in the red out-area, picks up the job, reads its next operation, (in this case blue), and moves the job to the in-area for the next operation. Eventually the blue operator colors in shells 5 through 8, and the job is moved to green, and finally to yellow. When the material handler notices that all operations are completed, he or she moves the job to the "Completed Jobs" stack.

Along with the routing information, each card also has a due date and a job number. The due dates are 1, 2, 3, or 4. They indicate relative due dates only. That is, jobs with due date 1 are due before due date 2 jobs, and so on. The job numbers range from 1 to 24 and are located in the lower right-hand corner of the shell. They are used only to identify the jobs.

Setup

The recorder should be stationed at the Completed Jobs stack, and records the "completion time" of each job as it is delivered. The operators and dispatchers should be seated, with each dispatcher-operator pair separated from the other three pairs. The material handlers do not require seats. The job shop is now ready to start. The recorder should note the time (minute and seconds) of the start. (It is most convenient to record this time as 0:00 and all other times as elapsed time from the start.)

Run

All of the jobs except jobs 19 and 24 are given to the material handlers, who distribute the jobs to the appropriate in-area for each job's first operation. Using the table in Figure 3, the recorder notes the time each job is placed in the Completed Job stack. Completion times should be measured as elapsed minutes and seconds (for example, 3 min, 32 seconds) since the demonstration started. As soon as two or three jobs have been completed (this usually takes about three or four minutes), the two remaining jobs (19 and 24) are released into the shop, with the announcement that job 24 is to be expedited (Job 24's due date is "EXPEDITE"). The recorder records the time these jobs are released. The shop continues until all jobs are completed. This usually takes about 5 or 6 more minutes.

Review
Go over the completion times and completion order. Calculate the flow times (completion time - release time) for jobs 19 and 24.

Experimentation
Suppose the exercise were changed. What would happen if....

1. More jobs were released?

2. Processing rate of the red machine was increased?

3. All the jobs were exactly the same?

4. All the jobs had exactly the same route (but different processing times)?

5. The variety of routes and processing times reduced?

Questions for Discussion

1. How did the dispatchers choose which job to do next? Did they use a formal rule? How did these decisions influence the results?

2. Compare the flow time of jobs 19 and 24. Why the difference?

3. What percentage of time was each workcenter idle? (Ask the operators and dispatchers for their estimates.) What factors not under the control of the dispatchers contributed to the amount of idle time? What factors under their control contributed to idleness?

4. If this demo were to be run again, but this time using dispatching rules that had to be followed instead of those arbitrarily used by a human dispatcher, what rules should be used?

SHELL GAME WORKSHEETS
JOBS RELEASED AT TIME 00:00

Job Number	Due Date	Completion Time	Order of Completion
1	2		
2	3		
3	1		
4	1		
5	1		
6	3		
7	3		
8	3		
9	3		
10	2		
11	3		
12	1		
13	1		
14	4		
15	3		
16	1		
17	4		
18	4		
20	1		
21	2		
22	2		
23	1		

JOBS RELEASED AT TIME _____

Job Number	Due Date	Completion Time	Order of Completion
19	4		
24	Expedite		

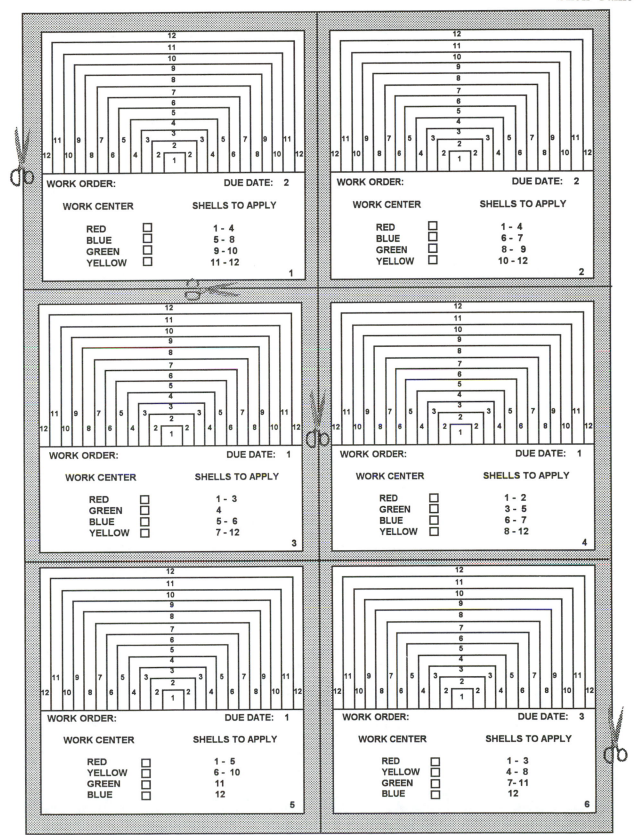

Card 1

WORK ORDER: DUE DATE: 2

WORK CENTER		SHELLS TO APPLY
RED	☐	1 - 4
BLUE	☐	5 - 8
GREEN	☐	9 - 10
YELLOW	☐	11 - 12

1

Card 2

WORK ORDER: DUE DATE: 2

WORK CENTER		SHELLS TO APPLY
RED	☐	1 - 4
BLUE	☐	6 - 7
GREEN	☐	8 - 9
YELLOW	☐	10 - 12

2

Card 3

WORK ORDER: DUE DATE: 1

WORK CENTER		SHELLS TO APPLY
RED	☐	1 - 3
GREEN	☐	4
BLUE	☐	5 - 6
YELLOW	☐	7 - 12

3

Card 4

WORK ORDER: DUE DATE: 1

WORK CENTER		SHELLS TO APPLY
RED	☐	1 - 2
GREEN	☐	3 - 5
BLUE	☐	6 - 7
YELLOW	☐	8 - 12

4

Card 5

WORK ORDER: DUE DATE: 1

WORK CENTER		SHELLS TO APPLY
RED	☐	1 - 5
YELLOW	☐	6 - 10
GREEN	☐	11
BLUE	☐	12

5

Card 6

WORK ORDER: DUE DATE: 3

WORK CENTER		SHELLS TO APPLY
RED	☐	1 - 3
YELLOW	☐	4 - 8
GREEN	☐	7 - 11
BLUE	☐	12

6

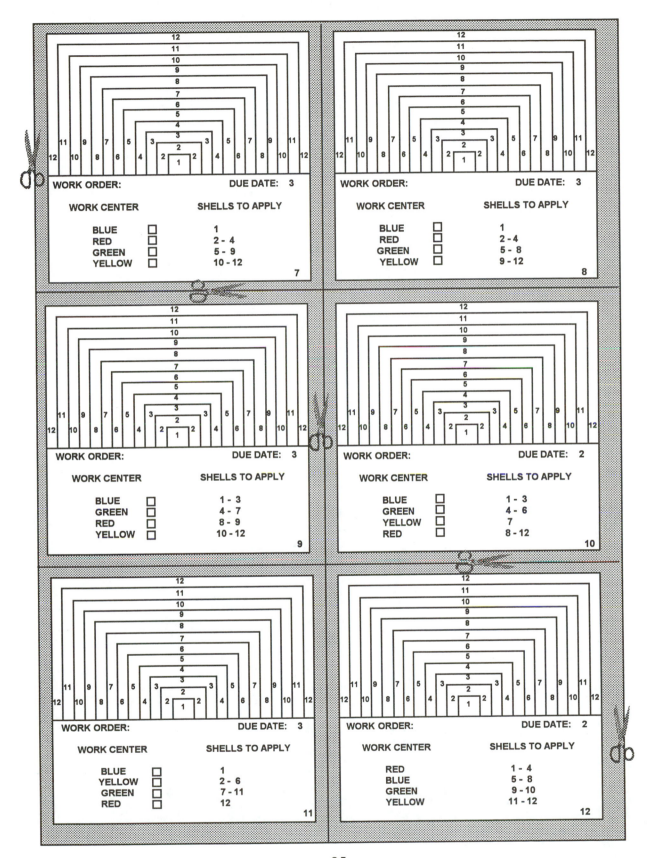

WORK ORDER: DUE DATE: 3

WORK CENTER		SHELLS TO APPLY
BLUE	☐	1
RED	☐	2 - 4
GREEN	☐	5 - 9
YELLOW	☐	10 - 12

7

WORK ORDER: DUE DATE: 3

WORK CENTER		SHELLS TO APPLY
BLUE	☐	1
RED	☐	2 - 4
GREEN	☐	5 - 8
YELLOW	☐	9 - 12

8

WORK ORDER: DUE DATE: 3

WORK CENTER		SHELLS TO APPLY
BLUE	☐	1 - 3
GREEN	☐	4 - 7
RED	☐	8 - 9
YELLOW	☐	10 - 12

9

WORK ORDER: DUE DATE: 2

WORK CENTER		SHELLS TO APPLY
BLUE	☐	1 - 3
GREEN	☐	4 - 6
YELLOW	☐	7
RED	☐	8 - 12

10

WORK ORDER: DUE DATE: 3

WORK CENTER		SHELLS TO APPLY
BLUE	☐	1
YELLOW	☐	2 - 6
GREEN	☐	7 - 11
RED	☐	12

11

WORK ORDER: DUE DATE: 2

WORK CENTER		SHELLS TO APPLY
RED		1 - 4
BLUE		5 - 8
GREEN		9 - 10
YELLOW		11 - 12

12

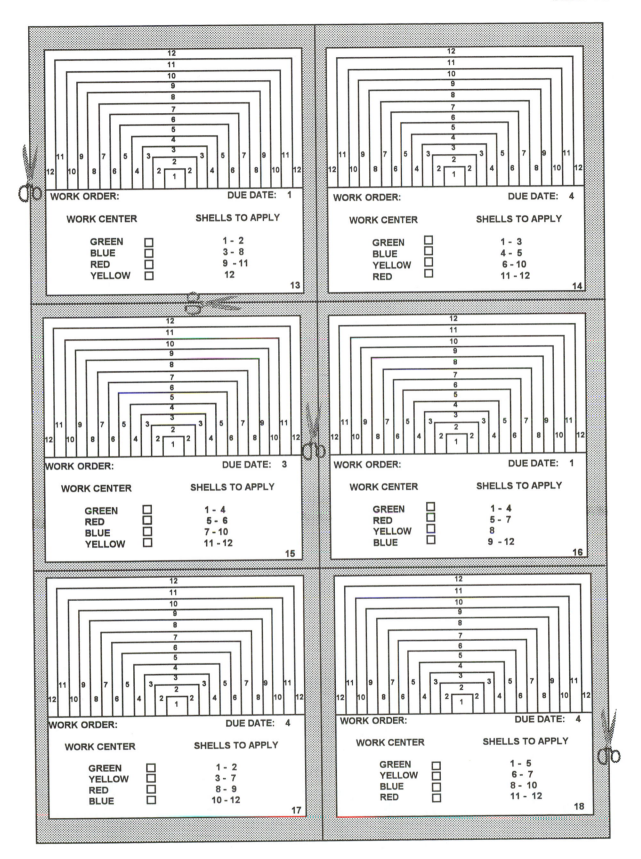

WORK ORDER: **DUE DATE:** 1	**WORK ORDER:** **DUE DATE:** 4
WORK CENTER **SHELLS TO APPLY**	**WORK CENTER** **SHELLS TO APPLY**
GREEN ☐ 1 - 2	GREEN ☐ 1 - 3
BLUE ☐ 3 - 8	BLUE ☐ 4 - 5
RED ☐ 9 - 11	YELLOW ☐ 6 - 10
YELLOW ☐ 12	RED ☐ 11 - 12
13	14

WORK ORDER: **DUE DATE:** 3	**WORK ORDER:** **DUE DATE:** 1
WORK CENTER **SHELLS TO APPLY**	**WORK CENTER** **SHELLS TO APPLY**
GREEN ☐ 1 - 4	GREEN ☐ 1 - 4
RED ☐ 5 - 6	RED ☐ 5 - 7
BLUE ☐ 7 - 10	YELLOW ☐ 8
YELLOW ☐ 11 - 12	BLUE ☐ 9 - 12
15	16

WORK ORDER: **DUE DATE:** 4	**WORK ORDER:** **DUE DATE:** 4
WORK CENTER **SHELLS TO APPLY**	**WORK CENTER** **SHELLS TO APPLY**
GREEN ☐ 1 - 2	GREEN ☐ 1 - 5
YELLOW ☐ 3 - 7	YELLOW ☐ 6 - 7
RED ☐ 8 - 9	BLUE ☐ 8 - 10
BLUE ☐ 10 - 12	RED ☐ 11 - 12
17	18

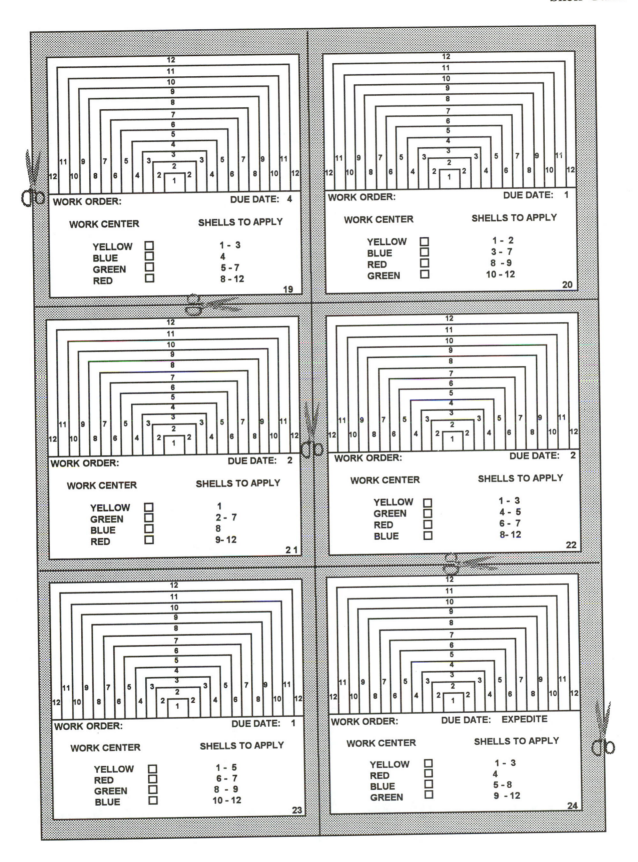

Card 19

WORK ORDER: DUE DATE: 4

WORK CENTER		SHELLS TO APPLY
YELLOW	☐	1 - 3
BLUE	☐	4
GREEN	☐	5 - 7
RED	☐	8 - 12

Card 20

WORK ORDER: DUE DATE: 1

WORK CENTER		SHELLS TO APPLY
YELLOW	☐	1 - 2
BLUE	☐	3 - 7
RED	☐	8 - 9
GREEN	☐	10 - 12

Card 21

WORK ORDER: DUE DATE: 2

WORK CENTER		SHELLS TO APPLY
YELLOW	☐	1
GREEN	☐	2 - 7
BLUE	☐	8
RED	☐	9 - 12

Card 22

WORK ORDER: DUE DATE: 2

WORK CENTER		SHELLS TO APPLY
YELLOW	☐	1 - 3
GREEN	☐	4 - 5
RED	☐	6 - 7
BLUE	☐	8 - 12

Card 23

WORK ORDER: DUE DATE: 1

WORK CENTER		SHELLS TO APPLY
YELLOW	☐	1 - 5
RED	☐	6 - 7
GREEN	☐	8 - 9
BLUE	☐	10 - 12

Card 24

WORK ORDER: DUE DATE: EXPEDITE

WORK CENTER		SHELLS TO APPLY
YELLOW	☐	1 - 3
RED	☐	4
BLUE	☐	5 - 8
GREEN	☐	9 - 12

The Beer Distribution Game

Topic Logistic supply chains, system dynamics

Purpose To introduce participants to the supply chain concept and to the effects decisions along the chain have on inventory levels and costs.

Introduction In this game the retailer sells cases of beer to a consumer and orders cases of beer from the wholesaler; the wholesaler sells cases of beer to the retailer and orders cases of beer from the distributor; and the distributor sells cases of beer to the wholesaler and orders beer from the factory (brewery). The factory brews the beer. For each week of play, every participant follows the same cycle *in this order and concurrently*:

1. Receive shipments and advance shipping delays,
2. Ship cases of beer according to new orders and backlog, subject to inventory availability,
3. Count inventory of cases of beer,
4. Advance the order slips (or brew), and
5. Place orders for (or brew) more beer.

There are only two costs involved in this simplified version of a logistics supply chain: inventory holding costs ($0.50/case/week) and backorder costs ($1.00/case/week). Each team has the goal of minimizing the sum of those costs by balancing the cost of having inventory (inventory holding cost) with the cost of being out of inventory when a customer orders beer (backorder cost).

Each participant keeps track of his or her own costs. At the end of the game, the total game cost for the distribution system is the sum of the four individual participants' total costs (retailer cost + wholesaler cost + distributor cost + factory cost). The goal is to **minimize team costs**.

This exercise was developed at the Massachusetts Institute of Technology's Sloan School of Management by its System Dynamics Group and contributed by John D. Sterman, Professor of Management Science and Director, MIT System Dynamics Group.

Materials	Game board Poker chips, which each represent 10 cases of beer Bingo chips or pennies, which each represent one case of beer Position Worksheet Inventory Graph Order Graph

Participants	Four Positions:
	  Factory (brewery)
	  Distributor
	  Wholesaler
	  Retailer
	Each position may be played by one or a pair of participants.

Action	The game begins with a fully-loaded "pipeline" of cases of beer:

- 12 cases of inventory in each of the "current inventory" squares,
- 4 cases in each of the "production delay" squares,
- 4 cases in each of the "shipping delay" squares, and
- orders for 4 cases in each "order placed" and "incoming order" squares (these are placed face down so that other participants cannot anticipate their demand)

Each position can communicate orders in written form only. No other form of communication is allowed between positions.

There should be a supply of blank order slips at each position. A generous supply of chips should be placed at the "raw material" area near the factory.

Practice

Each position team is allowed "two weeks" of practice, then sets the game board back to its starting state. Play starts again and continues, with all participants following this five-step cycle:

1. Receive your incoming inventory

Receive from the second shipping delay square (the one associated with the entity from whom you ordered beer) into your current inventory. You do this by advancing the chips from one square to the next. The Brewer receives from the closest production delay into your current ("finished") inventory.

Next, advance the cases of beer in the first shipping or production delay square to the second shipping or production delay square.

2. Fill (ship) orders.

Look at the order in your "incoming orders" square and look at your backlog on the Participant Worksheet. Fill all incoming orders plus backlog, if you can. To "Fill" orders, move chips from "current inventory" to the first shipping delay, or in the case of the retailer, to the "orders sold" square.

If your inventory is insufficient, fill as many orders as you can and add the remaining unfilled order amount to your backlog. You *may not* ship more beer than what is ordered from you plus what is in your backlog.

For example, if your current inventory is 1 case and your backlog is zero, after you fill an order for 4 cases you will have an inventory of zero and a backlog of three cases.

3. Count and record status — current inventory and backlog.

Record your current inventory or backlog on the Participant Worksheet. Note: You will never have cases in both current inventory and backlog.

4. Advance order cards.

Move the order cards (remember — face down!) from the "orders placed" to the "incoming orders" square. Factories initiate production by turning over the "production requests" card and introducing the requested beer into the top production delay.

5. Place orders.

Write your order quantity on an order card and place it face down on the "orders placed" square. Brewers place chips in the first "production delay" square. Brewery capacity is unlimited, so brewers may produce as much beer as they desire.

Record your order on the worksheet.

Go to Step 1

End of Play

Complete Inventory Graph and Order Graph (these may be provided on transparencies by your instructor).

Calculate the costs incurred at each position. Inventory costs are $0.50/case/week and backlog costs are $1.00/case/week. Sum the costs of each position to obtain a total team cost.

Questions for Discussion

About System Dynamics

1. Did you feel yourself controlled by forces in the system from time to time?

2. Did you find yourself "blaming" the person next to you for your problems?

3. What accounts for the dramatic fluctuations in the inventory levels? How might these fluctuations be mitigated.

About the Distribution Chain

1. What, if anything, is unrealistic about this game?

2. How would you determine the cost of holding inventory?

3. How would you determine the cost of a backorder?

4. Why are there order delays?

5. What occurs in the chain when a "customer" places an order?

6. Why are there production delays? Shipping delays?

7. Why have both distributors and wholesalers? Why not ship beer directly from the factory to the retailer?

8. Must the brewer be concerned with the management of the raw materials suppliers? If so, why? How can the suppliers affect the brewing process? Who manages the suppliers?

9. How was the capacity of the brewery determined? Is there much flexibility in the capacity?

10. Should an inventory policy be used? If so, what should it be?

Figure 1: Beer Distribution Game Board Set-Up

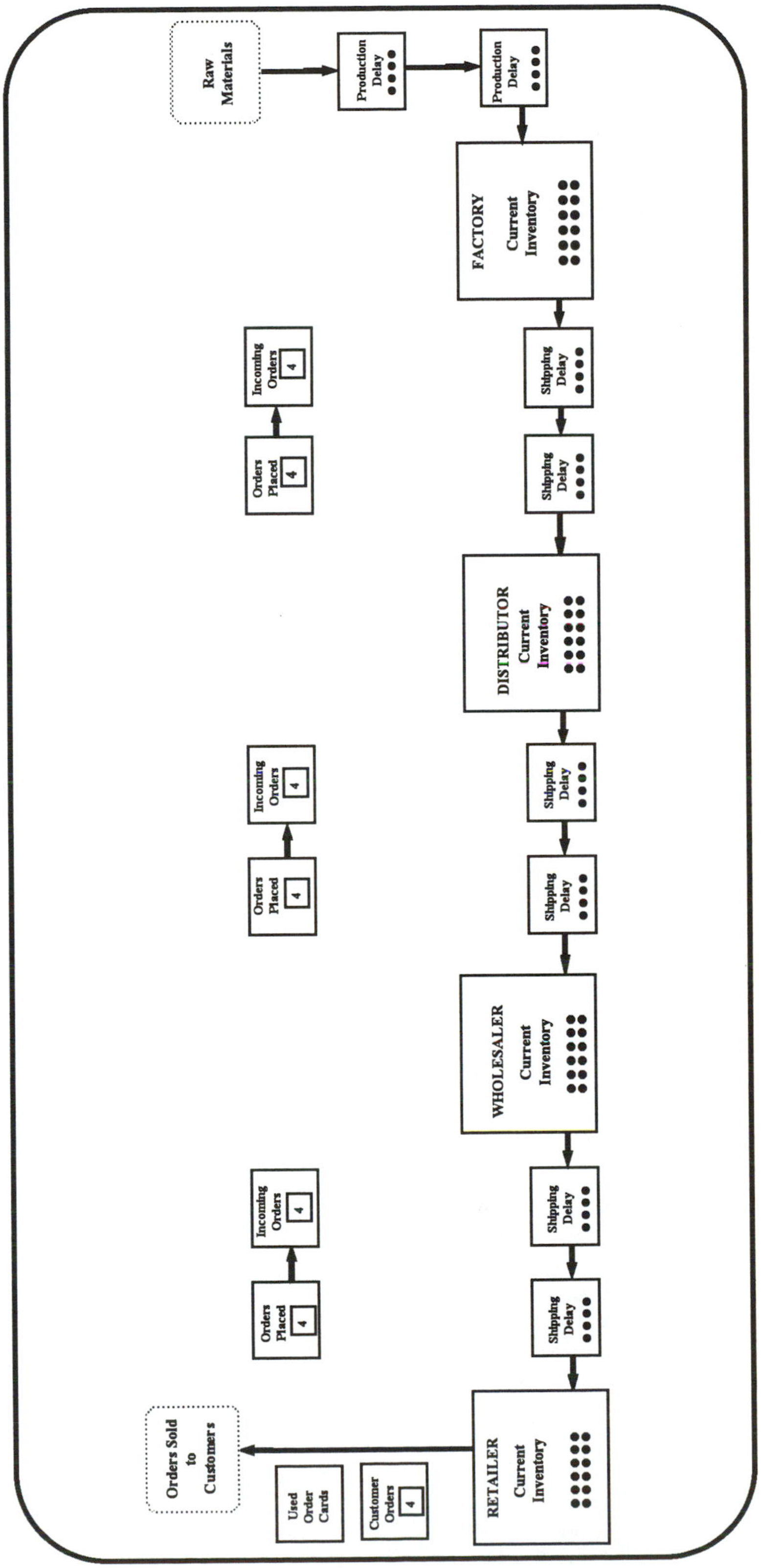
Raw Materials
Production Delay
Production Delay
FACTORY Current Inventory
Shipping Delay
Shipping Delay
Orders Placed 4
Incoming Orders 4
DISTRIBUTOR Current Inventory
Shipping Delay
Shipping Delay
Orders Placed 4
Incoming Orders 4
WHOLESALER Current Inventory
Shipping Delay
Shipping Delay
Orders Placed 4
Incoming Orders 4
RETAILER Current Inventory
Orders Sold to Customers
Used Order Cards
Customer Orders 4

POSITION WORKSHEET   Your Position: ____ Retailer ____ Wholesaler

Team Name _____   ____ Distributor   ____ Factory

Week	Inventory	Backlog	Orders
1			
2			
3			
4			
5			
6			
7			
8			
9			
10			
11			
12			
13			
14			
15			
16			
17			
18			
19			
20			
21			
22			
23			
24			
25			
Total			

Week	Inventory	Backlog	Orders
26			
27			
28			
29			
30			
31			
32			
33			
34			
35			
36			
37			
38			
39			
40			
41			
42			
43			
44			
45			
46			
47			
48			
49			
50			
Total			

TOTAL COST = (INV1 + INV2) * 0.5 + (BL1 + BL2) = _____

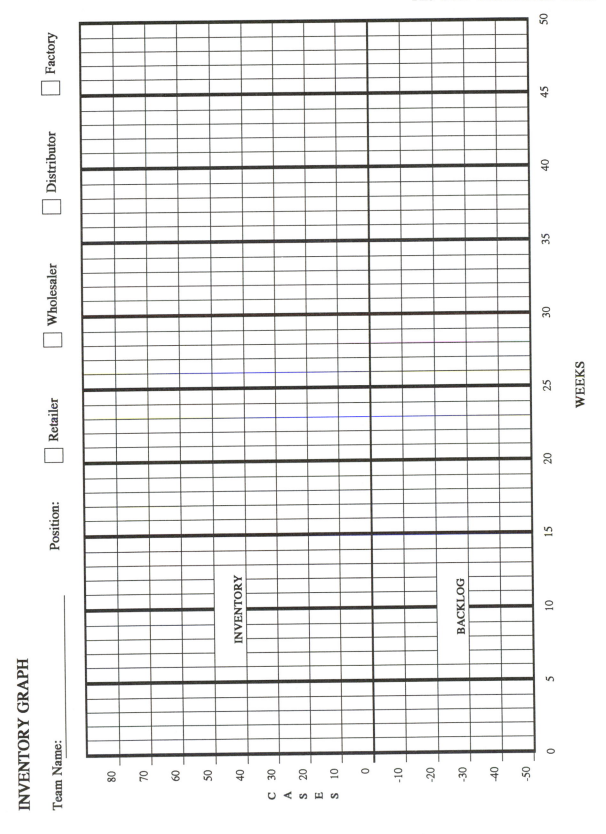

INVENTORY GRAPH

Team Name:

Position: ☐ Retailer   ☐ Wholesaler   ☐ Distributor   ☐ Factory

CASES

80
70
60
50
40
30
20
10
0
-10
-20
-30
-40
-50

INVENTORY

BACKLOG

WEEKS

0   5   10   15   20   25   30   35   40   45   50

ORDER GRAPH

Team Name: _____

Position: ☐ Retailer ☐ Wholesaler ☐ Distributor ☐ Factory

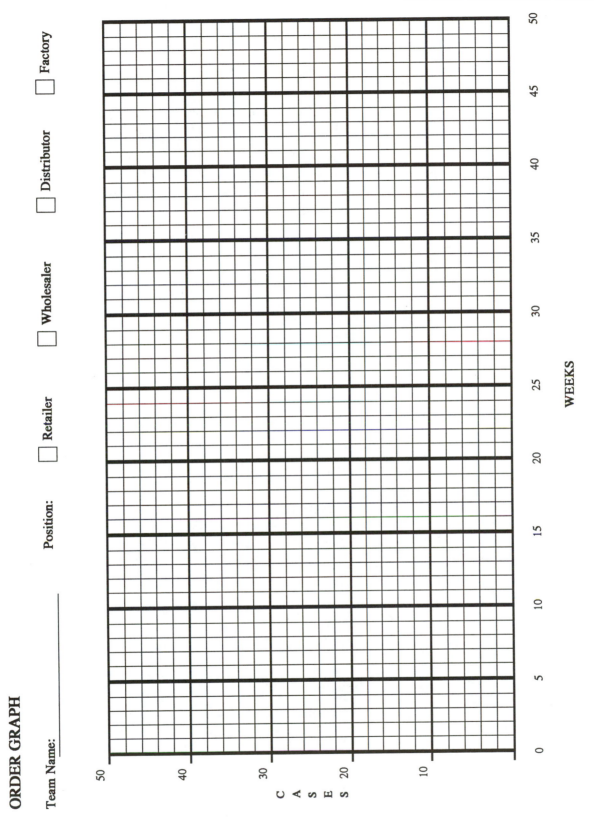

WEEKS

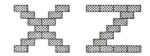

The Product X, Product Z Production Laboratory

Topic   Process analysis and production improvement

Purpose   This exercise provides an opportunity to measure production performance in a simulated assembly line production environment. It also provides an opportunity to reconfigure the process with the goal of improving throughput.

Introduction   The Production Laboratory has two main products, Product X and Product Z. Both products are a single-layer stack of LEGO® building blocks, assembled in a specific pattern. Engineering/manufacturing drawings of the products are supplied to the factory floor workers. (See the attached drawings.)

These products are built on a five-station production line. The current production process uses the batch production method with a transfer lot size (batch) of five units. The work to be accomplished at each work station is detailed in the Work Station Task Assignment document (Figure 1). The company is very concerned with the quality of its product, so every unit manufactured is thoroughly inspected and any errors corrected before shipment to the customer.

There is ongoing demand for both models and the likelihood that an order will be received for either product X or Z is equal, however, the order sizes vary considerably. Orders received by the company range in size in accordance with the demand distributions for Product X or Product Z shown in Table 1.

During the exercise, a random process is used to determine which product and what quantity to produce.

Regardless of the quantity demanded, material is transferred from inventory to the assembly work stations in lots of size five. For instance, if the order is for 15 units, three lots of five are released.

This exercise was created by Robert J. Schlesinger, Ph.D., Associate Professor of Information and Decision Systems, San Diego State University, San Diego, California.

Table 1: Demand Distributions

Order Size	Demand Distribution of Product X (Probability)	Demand Distribution of Product Z (Probability)
20 Units	.10	0
15 Units	.20	.20
10 Units	.30	.30
5 Units	.40	.50

To assess the performance of the process, it is necessary to collect accurate data on activity times, throughput, work in process (WIP), and product quality. The time taken to perform each stage is recorded by the Time Study Engineer. The resulting data should be used to perform a process and learning curve analysis. The Inventory Auditor keeps track of WIP in each buffer between work stations to assess throughput and WIP costs. These two people, in consultation with the Line Manager, should determine what data should be collected.

Players

17 players:
12 on the assembly line (five Material Handlers, five Assemblers, two Quality Control Inspectors, one for Product X and one for Product Z).

5 managers and staff (one Marketing Manager, one Purchasing and Material Control Manager, one Line Manager, one Inventory Accountant, and one Methods Study Engineer).

The instructor plays the roles of raw materials supplier and customer.

See Figure 2 for task assignments.

Materials

The production team needs:
LEGO® building blocks
A "Production Quantity Deck" (a standard deck of playing cards with all of the face cards and jokers removed)
Approximately 20 Production Order Forms with traveler tickets
4 or 5 End of Round Reports
A Stapler

Action

As a production team, you will have to decide how to lay out your assembly process. This should be completed before the session in which the activity will take place.

When the start of production is announced by your instructor, the Time Study Engineer will record the time in the End of Round Report. The production process is initiated by shuffling the Production Quantity Deck and withdrawing a card to determine which product will be produced and in what quantity. The table below indicates the resulting demand. (Be sure to replace the card and reshuffle before determining the next demand).

Table 2. Production Quantity Deck Correlations

Order Size	Product to Produce	
	Product X	**Product Z**
20 units	Black Ace	(Not an option)
15 units	Black 2 or 3	Red Ace or 2
10 units	Black 4, 5, or 6	Red 3, 4, or 5
5 units	Black 7, 8, 9, or 10	Red 6, 7, 8, 9, or 10

The next demand should be determined before the previous order is completed so that there will always be a backlog of demand.

After the demand for the first order has been determined, the marketing manager completes a Production Order Form and gives it to the factory Line Manager. The Line Manager fills in the required information, removes the traveler tickets, and passes the form on to the Purchasing/Material Control (P/MC) Manager. The P/MC Manager then procures the proper number, size, and color of raw material units from the supplier (instructor) in the correct lot size or lot size multiple. The Line manager issues the appropriate number of traveler tickets (one for each lot) to the Assembler at Work Station #1. Information and material then flows as shown in Figure 3.

The P/MC Manager releases raw material for a 5-unit lot to the first Material Handler. The Material Handler selects the number and type of parts required by the work station that he/she is supporting and

115

passes the remainder of the raw materials on to the next Material Handler, and so on, each withdrawing the materials needed by his/her work station. If the raw materials are not already separated from each other, the Material Handlers must dis-assemble the units to obtain the required parts. When all material for the order is dispersed, have the material handlers initial the Production Order Form and pass it to Q.C. Inspection.

Once Work Station #1 has the correct type and number of parts (at least for the first lot) and a traveler ticket authorizing production, the production assembly process begins. When Work Station #1 completes the lot of five units, Material Handler #1 moves the lot and its associated traveler ticket to Work Station #2. When Work Station #2 has the correct type and number of parts, the subassembly from Work Station #1, and the traveler ticket, assembly can commence. Similarly, each lot of five units then move down the line until the entire product has been assembled.

Each 5-unit lot is inspected as it is completed. Conforming product is shipped to the customer (returned to the instructor). If any unit is defective, the entire lot is rejected and the unit and its traveler ticket are passed backwards (from work station #5 to #4, to #3, etc.) up the line for rework. Each worker must inspect the unit to be sure that his/her task was performed correctly. When the error has been found, the reason is noted on the traveler ticket, and the unit is reworked. The repaired unit and the traveler ticket are returned to the quality control inspector. Once all lots have been inspected and accepted, the associated traveler tickets are stapled to the Production Order Form and the inspector then "signs off" that lot has been shipped to the customer.

When the last lot of an order has been completed at Work Station #1, the P/MC Manager can release material for the next order. The time the order is released to production should be noted on the Production Order Form. This cycle repeats for as many cycles as the instructor chooses.

The Time Study Engineer should note the time and enter it into the End of Round Report.

The instructor will stop the game. Completed orders will be credited to the company at $400 for each X unit and $300 for each Z unit. Material cost for the production of X and Z are $172 and $100 respectively. Work in process cost is calculated as follows (color is not a cost consideration):

8-peg blocks......$16 each
6-peg blocks......$12 each
4-peg blocks......$ 8 each

Labor cost will be treated as a percentage of the original labor configuration. For example, the initial "Production Flow Model" diagram shows 17 people. Wages and overhead for all employees is calculated at $60 per person per hour.

Experimentation

After the process has been run for a while using a lot size of five, re-run the exercise using progressively smaller lot sizes until you get to a lot size of one (JIT). Use the data gathered by the Time Study Engineer and the Inventory Auditor to assess any improvement (or deterioration) in the system's performance. Other process modifications may be allowed by your instructor.

Questions

1) What criteria would be useful for assessing the effectiveness and efficiency of an assembly process such as this?

2) What information would be required to measure these criteria?

3) How and where should such information be captured?

4) What factors affect process quality?

5) What is the effect of changing the lot size?

6) What changes to the process would you suggest?

7) What changes to the information flow would you suggest?

8) How would you assess the effects of these changes?

Figure 1. Work Station Assignments and Component Description

Production Model "X"

Work Station	Block #	Block Size	Block Color
#1	1	8	Red
	2	8	Red
	4	8	Blue
#2	3	6	Blue
	5	4	Blue
#3	6	8	Yellow
	7	8	White
	8	4	Yellow
#4	9	8	Blue
	10	4	Red
	11	8	Black
#5	12	4	Blue
	13	8	White

Production Model "Z"

Work Station	Block #	Block Size	Block Color
#1	1	6	Black
	2	4	Black
	4	6	White
#2	3	4	White
	5	6	Yellow
#3	6	4	Yellow
	7	4	White
#4	8	6	Red
#5	9	8	Black
	10	4	Red

Figure 2. Task Assignments

Marketing Manager: Marketing generates orders and markets time of delivery commitments to the customer. The order is passed to the Line Manager. Marketing is "graded" on how well the marketing schedule of delivery promises to customers is met.

Line Manager: The Line Manager has total responsibility for management and operation of the production process. The Line Manager reports directly to the President of the Production Laboratory (your instructor).

Purchasing/Material Control (P/MC) Manager: Reports to the Line Manager. The P/MC manager is responsible for seeing that raw material is passed to Material Handlers as soon as possible in the correct quantities, sizes, and colors.

Materials Handlers (5): Report to the Line Manager. They are responsible for providing the work stations with the material needed in the correct number, size, and color according to the lot size specified by the Line Manager.

Assemblers (5): Report to the Line Manager. Responsible for the manufacturing of the product in accordance with the specifications on the blueprints and in quantities specified by the P/MC on the traveler document.

Q.C. Inspectors (2): Report to the President of the Production Laboratory. Responsible for assuring the quality of the products shipped to the customer (one has primary responsibility for Product X, one for Product Z). They make recommendations for improving the product quality in the batch production mode. (This assignment will change under JIT.)

Inventory Auditor: Reports to the Line Manager. Keeps accounts on the number of units ordered by Marketing, the number of units shipped, the time of each shipment, and the number of lots rejected by Q.C. Works closely with the Time Study Engineer in the collection and preparation of data.

Time Study Engineer: Reports to the Line Manager. Collects data to calculate learning curves for the products. Also collects data so that throughput, WIP, and bottlenecks can be identified. Works closely with the Inventory Auditor on the collection of this data.

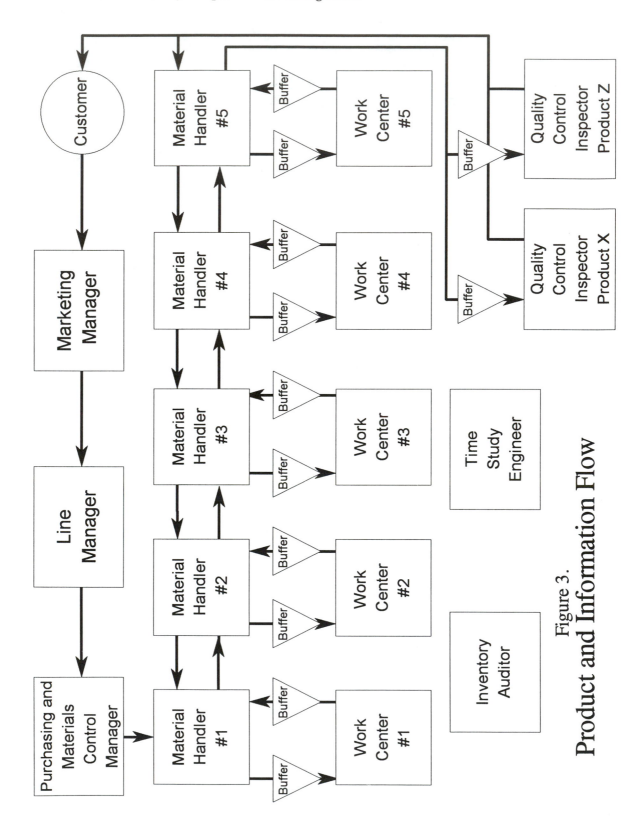

Figure 3.
Product and Information Flow

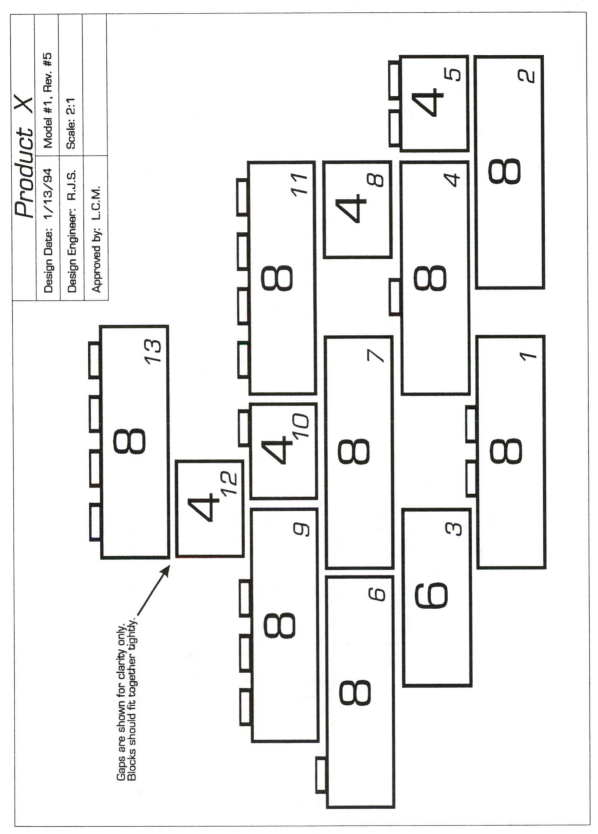

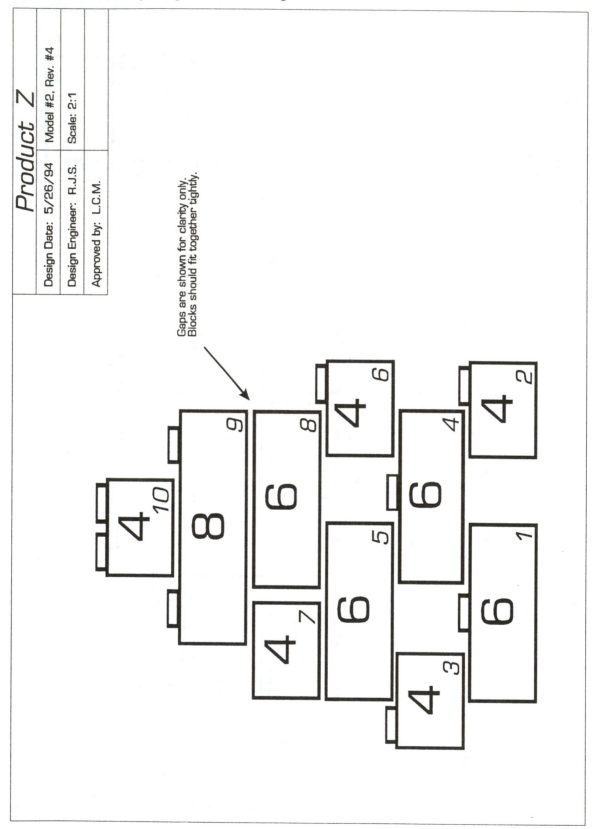

Gaps are shown for clarity only.
Blocks should fit together tightly.

The Product X, Product Z Production Laboratory

PRODUCTION ORDER FORM

MARKETING   Work Order #:_____   Time Order Placed: _____

Product: ☐ X   ☐ Z   Delivery Promise Time: _____

Quantity Required: _____

LINE   Lot Size: _____   Number of lots in this order (order size/lot size):   _____

MANAGER   Time Order Released to Production: _____

PURCHASING / MATERIAL

CONTROL   Time disbursement complete: _____

QC

MANAGER   Time FULL ORDER Shipped: _____

Traveler Tickets	Order # ____	Order # ____	Order # ____	Order # ____
	Lot # ____	Lot # ____	Lot # ____	Lot # ____
	☐ Accept	☐ Accept	☐ Accept	☐ Accept
Cut these lot travelers out.	☐ Reject	☐ Reject	☐ Reject	☐ Reject
	Reason for reject:	Reason for reject:	Reason for reject:	Reason for reject:
A lot traveler should accompany each lot as it moves through production	Lot Completion Time:_____	Lot Completion Time:_____	Lot Completion Time:_____	Lot Completion Time:_____
	Order # ____	Order # ____	Order # ____	Order # ____
	Lot # ____	Lot # ____	Lot # ____	Lot # ____
	☐ Accept	☐ Accept	☐ Accept	☐ Accept
	☐ Reject	☐ Reject	☐ Reject	☐ Reject
Staple completed travelers to Production Order Form.	Reason for reject:	Reason for reject:	Reason for reject:	Reason for reject:
	Lot Completion Time:_____	Lot Completion Time:_____	Lot Completion Time:_____	Lot Completion Time:_____

The Product X, Product Z Production Laboratory

End of Round Report

Total Number of Orders: _____

Total Units of Product X Ordered: _____

Total Units of Product Z Ordered: _____

Total Units of Product X Shipped: _____   X $400/unit = _____

Total Units of Product Z Shipped: _____   X $300/unit = _____

                                              Total Revenue = _____

Work In Process:

    8–Peg Blocks: _____   X $16/block = _____

    6–Peg Blocks: _____   X $12/block = _____

    4–Peg Blocks: _____   X $ 8/block = _____

                                                Total WIP = _____

Labor Costs:

    No. of Workers: _____

    Production time (minutes): _____

     Total Worker–Minutes _____

                               X $1/worker/minute = _____

                                   Resulting profit = _____

                                       / prod. time = _____ $/min

Comments:

Less is Better: Effects of Reduced Batch Sizes

Topic   Inventory management, lean production techniques

Purpose   This exercise illustrates the potential benefits of reducing production lot sizes. It begins with the Economic Order Quantity inventory model.

Introduction   A useful method for helping to decide on the most economic batch size is the Economic Order Quantity (EOQ) inventory model with a finite replenishment rate. When used for batch-size decisions, the model is variously known as the Economic Run Length (ERL) or Economic Lot Size Model (ELS).

Production line "A" produces ten different products. Each product has an annual demand of 18,000. Demand is steady and known. The production capacity is approximately 800 units per day. The line operates 250 days per year. Inventory holding costs average $8 per unit held, based on the average level of inventory level. A study has determined that the cost to switch from producing one type of product to another averages $202.22. Solving for ELS:

$$ELS = \sqrt{\left(\frac{2*DS}{H} * \frac{p}{p-d}\right)} = \sqrt{\left(\frac{2*18,000*202.22}{8} * \frac{800}{800-72}\right)} = 1,000$$

The results given by the model suggest to the production manager that the most economic decision is to produce in lot sizes of 1,000 for each of the 10 products. Regardless of which product is currently being produced, demand continues to occur for each of the nine other products which are not currently being produced. Therefore, the firm must hold enough stock of each of the other products to last until that product is next scheduled for manufacture.

This exercise was created by Donald G. Sluti, Ph.D., Assistant Professor of Production and Operations Management at the School of Business and Technology, University of Nebraska at Kearney.

Figure 1 shows inventory pallets, each holding 100 units of product. The Product A row, which has 10 pallets of 100 units each, represents the just-completed batch of 1,000 units. Each remaining row represents the demand for a product since its last scheduled run. The row which is down to its last pallet will be scheduled next for production.

Materials
Inventory Figure Worksheet

Players
General Manager (instructor)
All can participate

Action
The General Manager has decided that inventory levels must be dramatically reduced. In small groups, modify the equation above to reduce inventory by 50%. Redraw Figure 1 to illustrate the effect on inventory.

Questions for Discussion

1. In what ways can the ELS equation be modified to reduce inventory? What are the implications of each of the possible changes?

2. What are the benefits to the firm of reduced inventory?

Figure 1: Usual Inventory Levels

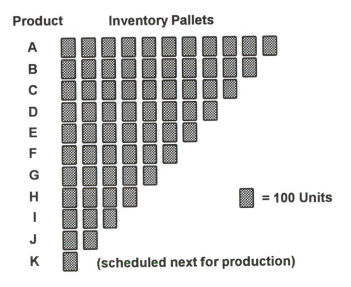

Inventory Figure Worksheet

Place an "x" over each pallet that holds inventory.

Cooperstown Cars, Inc.

Topic   Production Scheduling

A production schedule is a plan that determines *what* is to be produced, *how much* is to be produced and *when* it is to be produced. Production scheduling takes into account the demand for the product and the lead time (how long it takes from the time it is ordered to the time it is available.)

Purpose   The purpose of this exercise is to observe how the production schedule affects the flow of material through a production process where the product being manufactured is made up of subcomponents which, in turn, may also be made up of subcomponents). Among other things, the schedule will impact the efficiency and effectiveness of a production process. Efficiency may be assessed by how much extra inventory is injected into the system. Effectiveness may be gauged by how well production requirements are met.

Materials   A product tree describing the components (body, axles, and wheels) that make up the final assembly (a toy car) is shown in Figure 1. (Note that two axle assemblies are needed for each car and two wheels are needed for each axle assembly, so Figure 1 indicates that four wheels are needed for each car.)

Three copies of an Order Release/Receipt Matrix upon which to record the production activity, period by period, for the planning horizon of the exercise (See the Order Release/Receipt Matrix Worksheet).

Material Order Forms (see Figures 2A, 2B and 2C):
   You will schedule production in two passes. Each planner will need an order form for each of six to eight simulated planning periods per pass.

This exercise was contributed by Larry R. Dolinsky, Professor of Production and Operations Management at Bentley College, Waltham, Massachusetts. Credit is given to Peter Billington, Professor of Management at the University of Southern Colorado, Pueblo, Colorado, upon whose presentation this exercise is based.

Players   Four players per team:
                                   1 Body Planner
                                   1 Axle Planner
                                   1 Wheel Planner
                                   1 Schedule Auditor

Each planner is responsible for releasing orders, as he or she deems appropriate, so that the toy car company can meet customer orders. The schedule auditor records the activity as it occurs on the Order Release/Receipt Matrix worksheet.

Action   At the beginning of the exercise, your instructor will tell you how many toy cars will be demanded and when they will be required. You will also be given the lead time for each component: the time from when it is ordered until it becomes available for assembly. Keeping the end demand in mind, each production planner must decide how much material, if any, is to be ordered for each period. The quantity is written on the appropriate Material Order Release Form which is passed to the schedule auditor.

As each order form is collected, the schedule auditor places an *x* in the corresponding cell of the matrix, indicating that an order has been placed. The auditor also places the order quantity in a cell to the right of the *x* to indicate the lead time before the order will be received. For instance, if there is a two-week lead time, the order quantity will be recorded two time periods to the right of the *x* indicating the release of the order.

Whenever material which constitutes subassemblies of a component is received, the schedule auditor will assume that production of that component commences and will indicate the quantity produced in the appropriate row of the matrix, again offsetting (moving to the right) by the appropriate lead time. This will have to be done for completing the wheel assembly (when wheels and axles are available) and for final assembly (when axle assemblies and bodies are available).

This exercise is completed in two passes (see below). Play proceeds, period by period, until the planning horizon has been met (typically 6 to 8 periods).

At the end of the exercise, assess your team's performance by counting your excess inventory and how much demand for toy cars

132

was missed by how many periods. The smaller these numbers, the better your schedule worked.

First Pass — No consultation is to take place between the three materials planners. Each should independently determine the quantity to be ordered for each of the planning periods.

Second Pass — Discussion is allowed among the materials planners.

MRP Schedule — After both simulations have been run, you will develop, as a class, the MRP schedule.

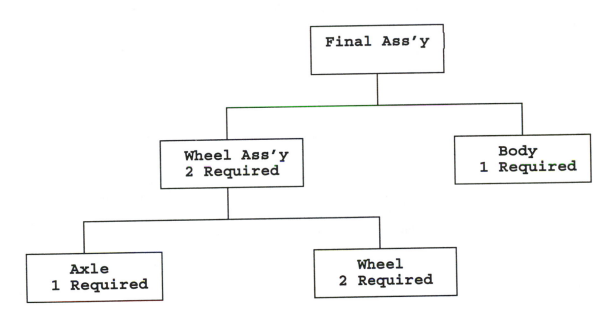

Figure 1. Product Tree

Questions for Discussion

After completing both passes and developing the MRP schedule, compare the MRP schedule to the schedules you created in the first two passes.

1) How is the information you exchanged in the second pass encoded in the MRP methodology?

2) What factors can you think of that will affect the number of toy cars you have to produce?

3) What factors will affect the number of sub-assemblies and basic components that you will need?

4) What information is necessary for the production planners to *effectively* plan order releases (in other words, make sure that demand is met)?

5) What information is necessary for the production planners to *efficiently* plan order releases (in other words, make sure that excess inventory is not carried)?

6) What elements of an MRP system provide the information needed to efficiently and effectively plan production orders? In other words, from where is the necessary information obtained?

Cooperstown Cars, Inc.

ORDER RELEASE/RECEIPT MATRIX WORKSHEET

First Pass: No Communication Among Materials Planners

Period →	1	2	3	4	5	6	7	8	9	10
Final Assembly										
Bodies										
Wheel Assembly										
Axles										
Wheels										

Second Pass: Materials Planners May Confer

Period →	1	2	3	4	5	6	7	8	9	10
Final Assembly										
Bodies										
Wheel Assembly										
Axles										
Wheels										

MRP Solution

Period →	1	2	3	4	5	6	7	8	9	10
Final Assembly										
Bodies										
Wheel Assembly										
Axles										
Wheels										

Material Order Form BODY Period 1 Quantity: _____	**Material Order Form** BODY Period 2 Quantity: _____
Material Order Form BODY Period 3 Quantity: _____	**Material Order Form** BODY Period 4 Quantity: _____
Material Order Form BODY Period 5 Quantity: _____	**Material Order Form** BODY Period 6 Quantity: _____
Material Order Form BODY Period 7 Quantity: _____	**Material Order Form** BODY Period 8 Quantity: _____

Material Order Form AXLE Period 1 Quantity: _____	**Material Order Form** AXLE Period 2 Quantity: _____
Material Order Form AXLE Period 3 Quantity: _____	**Material Order Form** AXLE Period 4 Quantity: _____
Material Order Form AXLE Period 5 Quantity: _____	**Material Order Form** AXLE Period 6 Quantity: _____
Material Order Form AXLE Period 7 Quantity: _____	**Material Order Form** AXLE Period 8 Quantity: _____

Material Order Form	Material Order Form
WHEEL	WHEEL
Period 1	Period 2
Quantity: _____	Quantity: _____

Material Order Form	Material Order Form
WHEEL	WHEEL
Period 3	Period 4
Quantity: _____	Quantity: _____

Material Order Form	Material Order Form
WHEEL	WHEEL
Period 5	Period 6
Quantity: _____	Quantity: _____

Material Order Form	Material Order Form
WHEEL	WHEEL
Period 7	Period 8
Quantity: _____	Quantity: _____

Gozinto Products

Topic   JIT production management and the use of Kanban methods

Purpose   The purpose of this exercise is to introduce the Kanban production control concept and to demonstrate its effect on quality and productivity.

Introduction In this exercise, workers at three Work Centers produce a product — called a gozinto — which consists of four playing cards secured together with a paper clip. Product specifications are:

1. The four cards must be of different suits (one spade, one club, one diamond, and one heart). The face value of the cards and the order in which the cards are stacked is immaterial.

2. Each card must be perfect — no cut corners or blemishes on the face of the cards will be accepted by the customer.

3. Each card must be facing in the same direction.

4. The paper clip must be affixed in the upper left hand corner of the face-side of the cards.

Materials   A deck of playing cards
Paper clips
Kanban Cards (See Figure 1)
Five containers, each large enough to hold either one subassembly or one finished product (such as a paper cup or diskette box).

Players   Five players:
Three players are responsible for assembling the product. Production Worker #1 combines one spade and one club to produce Subassembly A. Production Worker #2 adds one heart and one

---

This exercise was created by Peter Arnold, Ph.D., Associate Professor of Operations Management, J. Robb Dixon, Ph.D., Assistant Professor of Operations Management, and Jay S. Kim, Ph.D., Assistant Professor of Operations Management, Boston University School of Management, Boston, Massachusetts.

diamond to Subassembly A to yield Subassembly B. Production Worker #3 secures Subassembly B with a paper clip.

One Vendor, who is responsible for delivering the necessary inputs to the process.

One customer, who is responsible for taking delivery and evaluating the quality of received goods.

Action
Set-up

Seat the Production Workers next to each other at a table.
Work Center 1
One container
One Subassembly A Production Kanban
Eight playing cards (four spades and four clubs)

Work Center 2
Two containers
One Subassembly B Production Kanban
One Subassembly A Move Kanban
Eight playing cards (four hearts and four diamonds)

Work Center 3
Two containers
One Finished Product Production Kanban
One Subassembly B Move Kanban
Twelve Paper Clips

A worker may only perform an assembly operation if his or her work center possesses an empty container and a Production Kanban.

When a work center has an empty container and a Production Kanban:

1. The worker carefully reads the instructions on the Production Kanban and performs the work if all necessary materials are available.

2. If a subassembly is required, the worker places the appropriate Move Kanban into an empty container and turns to the upstream (supplying) work center. The worker then exchanges the Move Kanban with the supplying work center's Production Kanban leaving the empty container. Note: The subassembly is not removed from its original container.

3. The worker then performs assembly operation according to the instructions on the Production Kanban.

After start-up, production can only commence when the customer requests a unit of finished product.

Loading the system

Worker 1 takes his/her Production Kanban and assembles Subassembly A.

Worker #2 takes his/her Production Kanban, inserts the Move Kanban into the empty container, then turns to Work Center 1 and obtains Subassembly A, exchanging the empty container and Move Kanban for the container holding the subassembly. (Note: At this point Work Center 1 now has an empty container and a Production Kanban.) Worker #2 turns back to Work Center 2 and assembles Subassembly B.

Worker #1 has received a production signal (the empty container and a Production Kanban) and assembles a Subassembly A. Worker #1 places the subassembly in the empty container.

Worker #3 takes the Production Kanban, inserts the Move Kanban into the empty container, and turns to Work Center 2 and obtains Subassembly B in its container, leaving in its place the empty container with the Move Kanban. Worker #3 turns back to Work Center 3 and assembles the finished product. The finished product is placed in a container for finished goods.

(Note: At this point Work Center 2 now has an empty container and a Production Kanban. As Worker #3 turns back to his or her position, the Worker #2 notes the production signal and begins assembling a Subassembly B.)

The system is now completely loaded and ready for daily operations.

Introducing the Customer and the Vendor

The customer is responsible for:
   a. Requesting finished product directly from the process.
   b. Performing incoming inspection. (The instructor will provide detailed instructions to the Customer).

The vendor is responsible for:
    a. Delivering raw materials (playing cards) directly to the process in batches of four, one card of each suit.
    b. Acting as the representative of their company to the process.

Regular Operations

Regular operations commence when the customer requests a unit of production. Worker #3 delivers the unit to the customer and turns back to his or her Work Center with an empty container and a Production Kanban. Worker #3 then assembles a unit of finished product.

Continue the exercise for 8 to 12 iterations or until instructed to stop, being careful to maintain kanban discipline: work is done only when a Production Kanban and empty container exist.

Variations

Your instructor will introduce variations as the exercise continues.

Questions for Discussion

1. For each variation, how much time do workers spend idle? Is this good or bad? How might idle time be productively used by workers?

2. How should defective materials or errors in production be handled in this type of system?

3. What is the role of the supervisor/manager in this type of production system?

Figure 1: Kanban Cards

Work Center 1
Production Kanban
Subassembly A
Combine: 1 Spade with 1 Club

Work Center 1 ☞ 2
Move Kanban

Subassembly A

Work Center 2
Production Kanban
Subassembly B
Combine: 1 Heart with 1 Diamond

Work Center 2 ☞ 3
Move Kanban

Subassembly B

Work Center 3
Production Kanban
Finished Gozinto
Combine: 1 Subassembly A
with 1 Subassembly B

Cut these kanban apart for use in the Gozinto exercise.

Paper Hats:
A Two-Card (Dual) Kanban System
To Handle the Production of Multiple Products
at Multiple Workstations

Topic   JIT workload management, capacity management, and sequencing

Purpose   The purpose of this exercise is to demonstrate how production kanbans (P-Cards) and conveyance kanbans (C-Cards) are used to pull material through a production process.

Introduction   In this demonstration, three workstations will be used to produce four different kinds of paper hats in order-quantities of one. Both production and conveyance kanbans will be employed. *Kanban* is a Japanese word that means signal. In production, kanban are signals that initiate action. In this exercise, the signal to produce a hat (the production kanban) is a P-Card and the only time a product is produced is when a P-Card authorizes it. Likewise, the signal to convey a unit from one workstation to the next is a C-Card.

The product. The product is a paper hat sold in red or blue trim colors, with or without a star insignia. Each of the four products is produced on a make-to-stock (MTS) basis. As each unit is sold, kanbans pull another through the manufacturing process.

The process. In this demonstration, three workstations will be used to produce four different kinds of paper hats in order-quantities of one. Both production and conveyance kanbans will be employed.

Hats are produced at three workstations using production kanbans (P-Cards). Although every product follows the same routing (Workstation #1 $\Rightarrow$ Workstation #2 $\Rightarrow$ Workstation #3), the workstations are separated on the shop floor. Material handling between workstations is managed using conveyance kanbans (C-Cards). Material-Handler #1-2 conveys material between Workstation #1 and Workstation #2; Material-Handler #2-3 conveys material between Workstation #2 and Workstation #3. Figure 1 outlines the process.

This exercise was created by James Ward and Leroy B. Schwarz, Krannert Graduate School of Management, Purdue University.

Materials

A stack of 8½ x 11 inch paper (~ 100 sheets)
Kanban cards, 10 types (see Figure 2)
Paper clips
Blue and red markers
Adhesive stars (or paper stars and glue sticks)

Players/Action

There are six players in all: three at workstations, two materials handlers, and one customer.

General Instructions

No activity of any kind is to take place without a kanban card to authorize it. Sequencing of jobs should be first-come, first served. Each activity should stop if the right material is not available and remain idle until the right material is available.

The Customer. The customer follows the instructor's directions regarding "ordering" finished goods.

Workstation #1. Workstation #1 performs the basic fold, as detailed in Figure 3. Workstation #1 pulls on an unlimited supply of incoming raw material (8- 1/2 x 11 " paper) stored at its input area.

Since it has only one type of output, Workstation #1's workload is managed using a single type of P-Card. Before removing a unit from Workstation #1's output area, Material-Handler #1-2 removes its P-Card. This "free" P-Card authorizes Workstation #1 to produce another. After producing the fold, Workstation #1 attaches the work-in-process to the free P-Card that authorized its production with a paper clip and places the work-in-process and the P-Card together in its output area. (Since all of its outputs are the same, the production sequence at Workstation #1 doesn't matter.)

If there are no free P-Cards (if all its P-Cards are attached to units in its output area), Workstation #1 stops working and remains idle until a P-Card is freed.

Workstation #2. Workstation #2 trims each hat with red or blue by coloring in the "JIT" on the front of the hat, as shown in Figure 3.

Sequencing at Workstation #2 is First Come - First Served: that is, units are produced in the sequence their P-Cards have been freed. Workstation #2's workload is managed using two different types of P-

150

Cards, one for each color. As the material-handler removes output from Workstation #2's output area, he/she frees its P-Card. This authorizes Workstation #2 to produce another unit of that trim color. In order to produce another unit, Workstation #2 pulls incoming material from its input area after removing its C-Card. As C-Cards are freed they are left for pickup by Material-Handler #1-2. (This authorizes Material-Handler #1-2 to pull another unit from Workstation #1 's output area.) Workstation #2 then colors it, attaches the work-in-process to the P-Card that authorized its production with a paper clip, and places them together in its output area.

If there are no free P-Cards (if all its P-Cards are attached to units in its output area), then Workstation #2 stops working and remains idle until a P-Card is freed. Further, if Workstation #2 requires material but none is available in its input area, then he/she stops working and remains idle until a unit of required material becomes available.

Material-Handler #1-2. Material-Handler #1-2 is dedicated to conveying material between Workstation #1 and Workstation #2, using a single type of C-Card. Whenever Workstation #2 pulls material from its input area, a C-Card is freed. This authorizes Material-Handler #1-2 to convey it to Workstation #1's output area. If a unit of material is available there, he/she detaches its P-Card (thereby authorizing Production of another), attaches the unit to the C-Card with a paper clip and returns them together to Workstation #2's input area. Material-Handler #1-2 conveys only one C-Card (either with or without a unit attached) at a time. The sequence of conveyance is First Come - First Served; that is, the sequence in which C-Cards have been freed by Workstation #2. If there are no free C-Cards, then Material-Handler #1-2 stops working and remains idle until a C-Card is freed. Further, if there are no available units in Workstation #1's output area when Material-Handler #1-2 arrives there, then he/she stops working and remains idle until the required material becomes available.

Workstation #3. Workstation #3 completes folding each hat and, if specified, applies a star insignia. Workstation #3's workload is managed using four different types of P-Cards, one type for each of its four different outputs: Red with Star, Red without Star, Blue with Star, and Blue without Star. P-Cards are freed as units are sold from finished-goods inventory, which is Workstation #3's output area. Each free P-Card authorizes Workstation #3 to produce another unit, following a First Come - First Served sequence. After producing it, Workstation #3 attaches the P-Card that authorized its production and places them together into finished-goods inventory. In order to produce another unit Workstation #3 pulls incoming material from its input area — either a Red or Blue unit — after removing its C-Card. (This authorizes Material-Handler #2-3 to pull another unit of that color from Workstation #2's output area.) If there are no free P-Cards (if all of its P-Cards are attached to completed hats), then Workstation #3 stops working and remains idle until a P-Card is freed. Further, if Workstation #3 requires material that is not available in its input area, then he/she stops working and remains idle until a unit of required material becomes available.

Material-Handler #2-3. Material-Handler #2-3 is dedicated to conveying material between Workstation #2 and Workstation #3, using either a Blue or a Red C-Card. In particular, whenever Workstation #3 pulls material from its input area, a red or blue C-Card is freed. This authorizes Material-Handler #2-3 to convey it to Workstation #2's output area. If a unit of the right material is available there, he/she detaches its P-Card (thereby authorizing production of another), attaches the C-Card, and returns them together to Workstation #3's input area. Material-Handler #2-3 conveys only one C-Card (either with or without a unit attached) at a time. The sequence of conveyance is First Come — First Served: that is, the sequence in which C-Cards were freed by Workstation #3. If there are no free C-Cards, then Material-Handler #2-3 stops working and remains idle until a C-Card is freed. Further, if a unit of the required material isn't available in Workstation #2's output area when Material-Handler #2-3 arrives there, then he/she stops working and remains idle until the required material becomes available.

Questions for Discussion

Discussion About Set-up

1. Why should production stop:
   (a) if all P-cards are full?
   (b) if the right material isn't available in the workstation's input area?

2. Why should conveyance stop:
   (a) if all C-cards are full?
   (b) if the right material isn't available in the up-stream output area?

3. Why produce one unit at a time? What if a set-up takes time or costs money?

4. Why convey one card at a time? What if the conveyance has capacity for more?

5. Why are the workstations separated? Would C-cards be required if workstations were located next to one another?

6. If workstations were located next to one another:
   (a) How might production of another unit be signaled to upstream workstation?
   (b) Is the result a JIT system or an un-paced flow line?

7. Does sequence really not matter at WS#1 and MH#1-2?

8. On the number of kanbans:
   (a) Why are there 10 units of finished-goods inventory at WS#3? Why aren't there zero? Why weren't there 14?
   (b) Why are there 3 units of each red but only 2 units of each blue in finished-goods inventory?
   (c) Why are there 4 units in WS#2's input area? Why 2 units of each?
   (d) Why are there 2 units in WS#1's output area? Why not 3 or 1?
   (e) What's the difference between inventory in WS#2's output area and inventory in WS#3's input area?

Discussion About What Happened
1. What happened when customer demand stopped?
   (a) Is it desirable for production to stop if slackening of demand is due to randomness?
   (b) How can management level workload if demand is basically level but random?
   (c) How can management level workload if demand is seasonal?

2. What happened when the conveyance stopped working?
   (a) Is it desirable for all production to stop if one activity is disabled?
   (b) What if one or more activities are periodically disabled (e.g. maintenance)?

3. What happened when the customer arrived for 25 hats?
   (a) What happened when the customer announced his order for 25 hats?
   (b) What should have happened? How might management have made it happen?

Experimentation

"What If" Discussion

1. What if Workstation #1 doesn't have an unlimited supply of material:
   (a) if material is provided by another cell or workcenter in the plant?
   (b) if material is provided by an outside supplier?

2. What if the process can only produce in batches of 6 units each (and batches take 6 times longer to produce than a single unit)?

3. What if finished goods are sold at a retail store located in another city?

4. What if the same conveyance plays the roles of both MH#1-2 and MH#2-3.

5. What if MH#2-3 is only available 4 hours during each 8-hour production day?

6. What if changeovers are required at WS#2 every time it changes color?

7. What if management would like to increase the variety of products offered to customers:
   (a) by offering hats with 2 stars (in addition to none and 1)?
   (b) by offering a second paper color?

Figure 1: The Process for Making Paper Hats

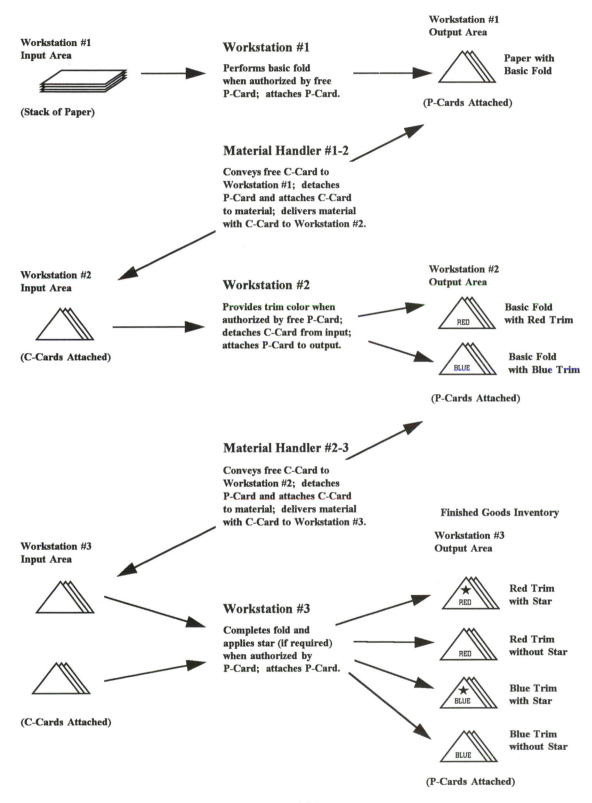

Figure 2: Kanban Cards

Ten different types of kanban cards are used in the Kanban demonstration. The cards are attached to the corresponding work-in-process or finished goods using paper clips.

P-Card for Workstation #1

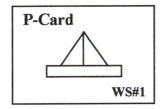

C-Card for Material Handler #1-2

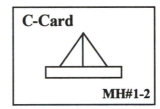

P-Cards for Workstation #2

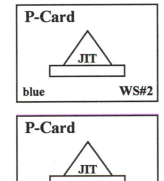

C-Cards for Material Handler #2-3

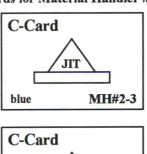

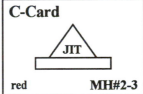

P-Cards for Workstation #3

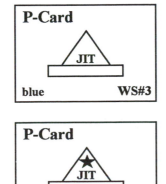

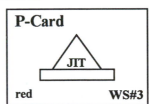

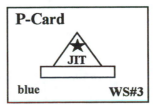

JIT

OPERATIONS

MANAGEMENT

Step 1: Fold Here

Step 2: Fold In

159

Yokimabobs

Topic

Kanban/JIT production

Purpose

The purpose of this game is to demonstrate the basics of Kanban/Just-In-Time (JIT) production, in a hands-on manner, to a relatively small group of people. The game shows how inventory is reduced in a JIT system until it reaches the minimum level necessary to keep up with demand.

Introduction

The game consists of a three-stage production process which assembles Yokimabobs. Yokimabobs come in 3" and 4" models. Each model consists of parts (bolts, nuts, and washers) that are assembled into components (Thingas and Majigs) at the first Workstation. The components are assembled into Yokis and Mabobs at Workstation 2. At Workstation 3, Yokimabobs are made by coupling a Yoki to a Mabob, hence the name (See Figures 1 & 2). Production is controlled by a 2-Card kanban system: Production Kanban (PK) and Move Kanban. In this exercise, there are two types of Move Kanban: Move Kanban (MK) are for components and subassemblies and Supply Kanban (SK) are for parts. The kanban cards always accompany the containers that hold parts, components, subassemblies, and finished goods, so the containers/kanban are referred to as kanban throughout the exercise.

The action starts when the customer withdraws a 4" Yokimabob container from Workstation 3. A Production Kanban signals the worker in Workstation 3 to produce 4" Yokimabobs to replace the ones taken by the customer, and to generate a Move Kanban. The worker in Workstation 2 begins to produce 4" Yokis and 4" Mabobs to replenish those used by the worker in Workstation 3. In turn, the worker in Workstation 1 must produce 4" Thingas and 4" Mabobs to replace those used at Workstation 2. While all of this activity is going on, suppliers to the three stations are being signalled with Supply Kanban to replenish the parts that have been used.

Next the customer withdraws a container of 3" Yokimabobs, which are slightly simpler to make, and the whole process repeats itself.

This exercise was created by Robert E. Stein, CASE Design, Inc. and Conor F. O'Muirgheasa, Teaching Fellow, University of Houston, Houston, TX.

Materials

> Kanban Cards
> Inventory Counts Sheet

Hardware

2½" Hex Bolt	100 (1 Box)
2" Hex Bolt	100 (1 Box)
1" Hex Bolt	100 (1 Box)
¾" Hex Bolt	100 (1 Box)
Cut Washers	5 lbs. (1 Box)
Hex Nuts	700 (7 Boxes)
Rod Coupler	50

30 - Drawer Organizer   3

Players

13 Players:
- 1 Customer
- 1 Marketing Person, who lets Worker 3 know that finished goods need to be replaced
- 1 Mover
- 1 Bolt Supplier
- 1 Coupler Supplier
- 1 Nut Supplier
- 1 Washer Supplier
- 3 Workers (One each at Workstations 1, 2, and 3)
- 3 Disassemblers

Action

Before you read this section, carefully review the Workstation Layout in Figure 3. Note that each Workstation is divided into three sections: Inbound, which holds inventory that will be used for assembly at that Workstation; Processing, where production takes place; and Outbound, where output from that Workstation is placed. Refer to Figure 3 as you read each Player's tasks and follow the movement through the system. The steps may seem confusing at first, but if you walk through them on Figure 3, the procedure becomes quite clear.

Set-up

The action begins with a "loaded system" as indicated in the "Initial Count" column of the Inventory Counts Sheet and with the three Workstations organized as shown in Figure 3.

162

Basic Steps: 4" The Customer initiates the process by withdrawing a container of 5 Yokimabobs from the Produce 4" Yokimabobs Kanban (4" Yokimabob PK) at Workstation 3. As soon as the Customer withdraws the completed Yokimabobs, the Disassemblers should begin to take them apart all the way down to their elemental parts, then return these parts to their respective suppliers. The Marketing person then places the empty 4" Yokimabob PK in the Production Ordering Post.

When an empty 4" Yokimabob PK appears in the Production Ordering Post, Worker 3:

1. Takes the empty 4" Yokimabob PK from the Production Ordering Post and places it in the center of the production area and reads the Production Card.
2. Takes a Coupler Supply Kanban (Coupler SK) from the inbound side of Workstation 3 and empties its contents in the Workstation 3 Production Area.
3. Places the empty Coupler SK in the Workstation 3 Supply Ordering Post.
4. Takes a 4" Yoki Move Kanban (4" Yoki MK) from the inbound side of Workstation 3 and empties its contents in the Workstation 3 Production Area.
5. Places the empty 4" Yoki MK in the Workstation 3 Move Ordering Post.
6. Takes a 4" Mabob Move Kanban (4" Mabob MK) from the inbound side of Workstation 3 and empties its contents in the Workstation 3 Production Area.
7. Places the empty 4" Mabob MK in the Workstation 3 Move Ordering Post.
8. Assembles five 4" Yokimabobs.
9. Places the completed Yokimabobs in the 4" PK and places the PK in the outbound area of Workstation 3 (its original position).

When the empty Coupler SK arrives at the Supply Ordering Post, the Coupler Supplier puts five Couplers into the empty Coupler SK and places the now full Coupler SK in the inbound side of Workstation 3.

When the empty 4" Yoki and Mabob MKs arrive at the Move Ordering Post, the Mover:

1. Empties the contents of one 4" Yoki PK from the outbound area of Workstation 2 into the empty 4" Yoki MK from the Move Ordering Post of Workstation 3.

2. Places the now full 4" Yoki MK in the inbound side of Workstation 3.
3. Places the now-empty 4" Yoki PK in the Production Ordering Post in the outbound side of Workstation 2.
4. Empties the contents of one 4" Mabob PK from the outbound area of Workstation 2 into the empty 4" Mabob MK from the Move Ordering Post of Workstation 3.
5. Places the now full 4" Mabob MK in the inbound side of Workstation 3.
6. Places the now-empty 4" Mabob PK in the Production Ordering Post in the outbound side of Workstation 2.

When the empty 4" Yoki PK arrives at the Production Ordering Post, Worker 2:

1. Takes the empty 4" Yoki PK from the Production Ordering Post of Workstation 2, places it in the Production Area of Workstation 2, and reads the card.
2. Takes a Washer Supply Kanban (Washer SK) from the inbound side of Workstation 2 and empties its contents in the Workstation 2 Production Area.
3. Places the empty Washer SK in the Workstation 2 Supply Ordering Post.
4. Takes a Nut Supply Kanban (Nut SK) from the inbound side of Workstation 2 and empties its contents in the Workstation 2 Production Area.
5. Places the empty Nut SK in the Workstation 2 Supply Ordering Post.
6. Empties the contents of one 4" Thinga Move Kanban (4" Thinga MK) into the Workstation 2 Production Area.
7. Places the empty 4" Thinga MK in the Workstation 2 Move Ordering Post.
8. Assembles five 4" Yokis.
9. Places the completed Yokis in the 4" Yoki PK and places the 4" Yoki PK in the outbound area of Workstation 2 (its original position).

When the empty Washer SK arrives at the Supply Ordering Post, the Washer Supplier puts five Washers into the empty Washer SK and places the now full Washer SK in the inbound side of Workstation 2.

When the empty Nut SK arrives at the Supply Ordering Post, the Nut Supplier puts five Nuts into the empty Nut SK and places the now full Nut SK in the inbound side of Workstation 2.

164

When the empty 4" Mabob PK arrives at the Production Ordering Post, Worker 2:

1. Takes the empty 4" Mabob PK from the Workstation 2 Production Ordering Post, places it in the Production Area of Workstation 2, and reads the card.
2. Takes three Nut Supply Kanban (Nut SKs) from the inbound side of Workstation 2 and empties their contents in the Workstation 2 Production Area.
3. Places the empty Nut SKs in the Workstation 2 Supply Ordering Post.
4. Takes two Washer Supply Kanban (Washer SKs) from the inbound side of Workstation 2 and empties their contents in the Workstation 2 Production Area.
5. Places the empty Nut SKs in the Workstation 2 Supply Ordering Post.
6. Empties the contents of one 4" Majig Move Kanban (4" Majig MK) into the Production Area of Workstation 2.
7. Places the empty 4" Majig MK in the Move Ordering Post of Workstation 2.
8. Assembles five 4" Mabobs.
9. Places the completed 4" Mabobs in the 4" Mabob PK and places the 4" Mabob PK in the outbound area of Workstation 2 (its original position).

When the empty Washer SKs arrive at the Supply Ordering Post, the Washer Supplier puts five Washers into each of the empty Washer SKs and places the now full Washer SKs in the inbound side of Workstation 2.

When the empty Nut SKs arrive at the Supply Ordering Post, the Nut Supplier puts five Nuts into each of the empty Nut SKs and places the now full Nut SKs in the inbound side of Workstation 2.

When the empty 4" Majig and Thinga MKs arrive in the Move Ordering Post, the Mover:

1. Empties the contents of one 4" Majig PK from the outbound area of Workstation 1 into the empty 4" Majig MK from the Move Ordering Post of Workstation 2.
2. Places the now full 4" Majig MK in the inbound side of Workstation 2.
3. Places the now-empty 4" Majig PK into the Production Ordering Post in the outbound side of Workstation 1.

Games and Exercises for Operations Management

4. Empties the contents of one 4" Thinga PK from the outbound area of Workstation 1 into the empty 4" Thinga MK from the Move Ordering Post of Workstation 2.
5. Places the now full 4" Thinga MK in the inbound side of Workstation 2.
6. Places the now-empty 4" Thinga PK into the Production Ordering Post in the outbound side of Workstation 1.

When the empty 4" Thinga PK arrives in the Production Ordering Post, Worker 1:

1. Takes the empty 4" Thinga PK from the Workstation 1 Production Ordering Post in the Production Area of Workstation 1 and reads the card.
2. Takes one 1" Bolt Supply Kanban (1" Bolt SK) from the inbound side of Workstation 1 and empties its contents in the Workstation 1 Production Area.
3. Places the empty 1" Bolt SK in the Workstation 1 Supply Ordering Post.
4. Takes one Nut Supply Kanban (Nut SK) from the inbound side of Workstation 1 and empties its contents in the Workstation 1 Production Area.
5. Places the empty Nut SK in the Workstation 1 Supply Ordering Post.
6. Assembles five 4" Thingas
7. Places the completed 4" Thingas in the 4" Thinga PK and places the 4" Thinga PK in the outbound area of Workstation 1 (its original position).

When the empty 1" Bolt SK arrives in the Supply Ordering Post, the Bolt Supplier puts five 1" Bolts into the empty 1" Bolt SK and places the now full 1" Bolt SK in the inbound side of Workstation 1.

When the empty Nut SK arrives in the Supply Ordering Post, the Nut Supplier puts five Nuts into the empty Nut SK and places the now full Nut SK in the inbound side of Workstation 1.

When the empty 4" Majig PK arrives in the Production Ordering Post, Worker 1:

1. Takes the empty 4" Majig PK from the Workstation 1 Production Ordering Post in the Production Area of Workstation 1 and reads the card.

166

2. Takes one 2½" Bolt Supply Kanban (2½" Bolt SK) from the inbound side of Workstation 1 and empties its contents in the Workstation 1 Production Area.

3. Places the empty 2½" Bolt SK in the Workstation 1 Supply Ordering Post.

4. Takes three Nut Supply Kanban (Nut SKs) from the inbound side of Workstation 1 and empties their contents in the Workstation 1 Production Area.

5. Places the empty Nut SKs in the Workstation 1 Supply Ordering Post.

6. Takes two Washer Supply Kanban (Washer SKs) from the inbound side of Workstation 1 and empties their contents in the Workstation 1 Production Area.

7. Places the empty Washer SKs in the Workstation 1 Supply Ordering Post.

8. Assembles five 4" Majigs

9. Places the completed 4" Majigs in the 4" Majig PK and places the 4" Majig PK in the outbound area of Workstation 1 (its original position).

When the empty 2½" Bolt SK arrives at the Supply Ordering Post, the Bolt Supplier puts five 2½" Bolts into the empty 2½" Bolt SK and places the now full 2½" Bolt SK in the inbound side of Workstation 1.

When the empty Nut SKs arrive at the Supply Ordering Post, the Nut Supplier puts five Nuts into each of the three empty Nut SKs and places the now full Nut SKs in the inbound side of Workstation 1.

When the empty Washer SKs arrive at the Supply Ordering Post, the Washer Supplier puts five washers into each of the two empty Washer SKs and places the now full Washer SKs in the inbound side of Workstation 1.

Basic Steps: 3"   The Customer initiates the process by withdrawing a container of 5 Yokimabobs from the Produce 3" Yokimabobs Kanban (3" Yokimabob PK) at Workstation 3. Following the same production steps above, produce 3" Yokimabobs according to the directions on the Produce Kanban for 3" Yokimabobs.

Inventory Counts   After making one round of 4" Yokimabobs and 3" Yokimabobs, complete the Count 1 column on the Inventory Counts Sheet.

Experimentation

Reduce the materials and WIP inventory levels to 50% of the starting inventory levels and complete Column 2 on the Inventory Counts Sheet. Repeat the production process and complete Column 3 on the Inventory Counts Sheet.

Try to reduce the inventory still further. How can this be achieved? Complete Column 4 on the Inventory Counts Sheet. Repeat the production process and complete Column 5 on the Inventory Counts Sheet. Calculate the percentage change in total inventory for each pass.

Questions for Discussion

1. What "drives" the Yokimabob production process?

2. Where was the bottleneck in this process? How could the bottleneck be addressed? Once you have addressed this bottleneck, what might you expect to happen?

3. What is the function of the Move and Produce Kanban Cards?

Figure 1: Yokimabob Parts, Components, Subassemblies, and End Products

Parts

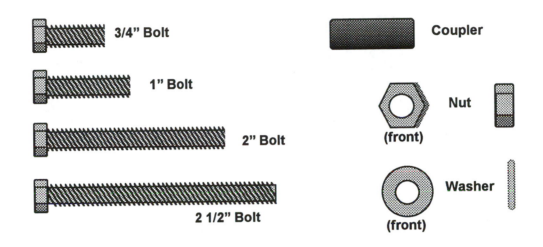

3/4" Bolt

1" Bolt

2" Bolt

2 1/2" Bolt

Coupler

Nut (front)

Washer (front)

Components: Thingas and Majigs

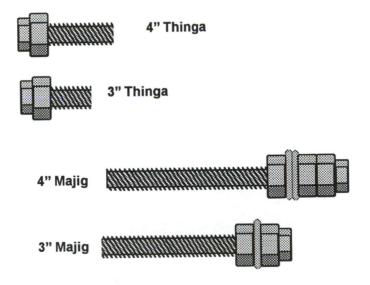

4" Thinga

3" Thinga

4" Majig

3" Majig

169

Figure 1: Yokimabob Parts, Components, Subassemblies, and End Products
(continued)

Subassemblies: Yokis and Mabobs

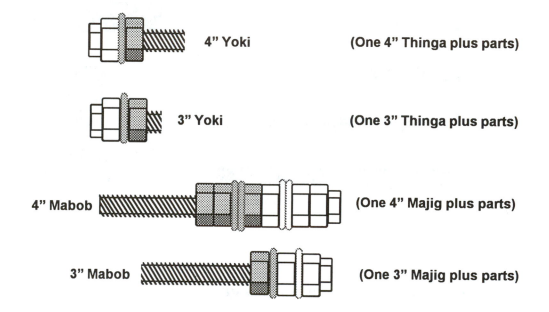

4" Yoki   (One 4" Thinga plus parts)

3" Yoki   (One 3" Thinga plus parts)

4" Mabob   (One 4" Majig plus parts)

3" Mabob   (One 3" Majig plus parts)

End Products: Yokimabobs

(One 4" Yoki plus one 4" Mabob)

(One 3" Yoki plus one 3" Mabob)

170

Figure 2: Yokimabob Product Structure Trees

Product Structure Tree for 4" Yokimabob

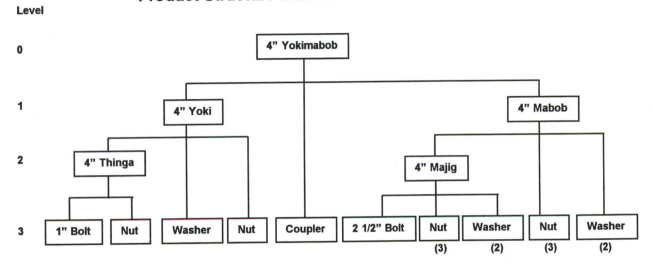

Product Structure Tree for 3" Yokimabob

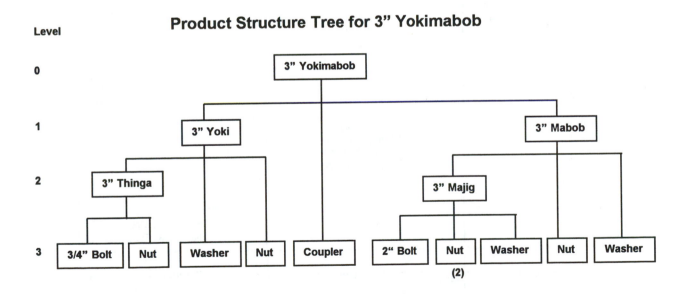

Note: All quantities are one, unless indicated in parentheses below the item.

171

Figure 3: Yokimabob Process and Workstation Layouts

Process Layout

Workstation 1	Workstation 2	Workstation 3

Each of the three tables should be approximatley five feet long.
The tables should be placed about five feet apart.

Layout for Workstation 1

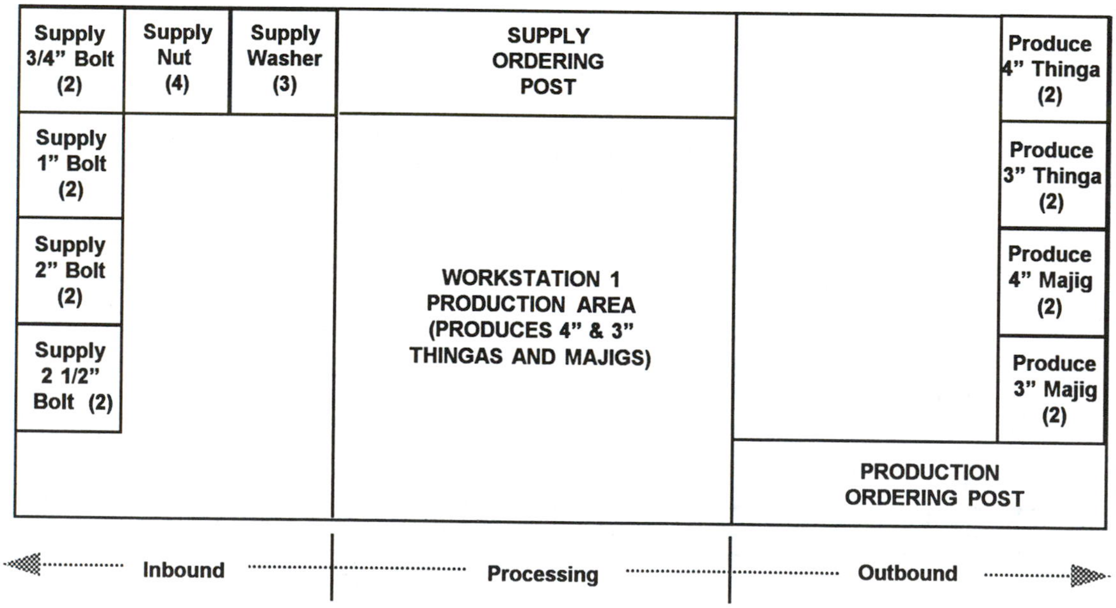

Supply 3/4" Bolt (2)	Supply Nut (4)	Supply Washer (3)	SUPPLY ORDERING POST		Produce 4" Thinga (2)
Supply 1" Bolt (2)					Produce 3" Thinga (2)
Supply 2" Bolt (2)			WORKSTATION 1 PRODUCTION AREA (PRODUCES 4" & 3" THINGAS AND MAJIGS)		Produce 4" Majig (2)
Supply 2 1/2" Bolt (2)					Produce 3" Majig (2)
				PRODUCTION ORDERING POST	

◄┅┅┅ Inbound ┅┅┅┅┼┅┅┅ Processing ┅┅┅┼┅┅┅ Outbound ┅┅┅►

Numbers in parentheses indicate number of containers/kanban.

Figure 3: Yokimabob Process and Workstation Layouts
(continued)

Layout for Workstation 2

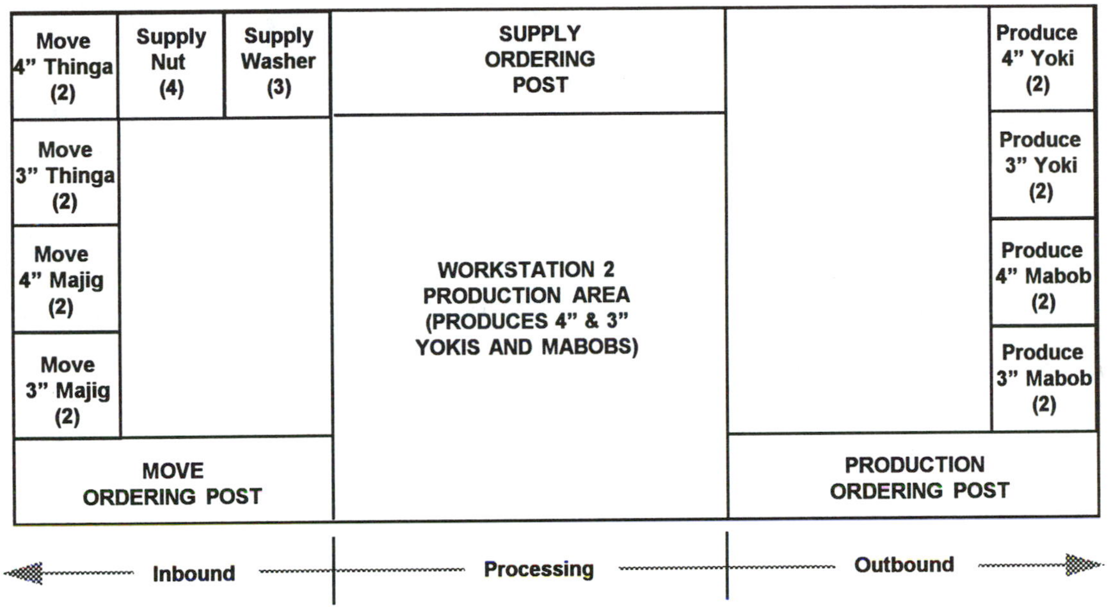

Move 4" Thinga (2)	Supply Nut (4)	Supply Washer (3)	SUPPLY ORDERING POST		Produce 4" Yoki (2)
Move 3" Thinga (2)					Produce 3" Yoki (2)
Move 4" Majig (2)			WORKSTATION 2 PRODUCTION AREA (PRODUCES 4" & 3" YOKIS AND MABOBS)		Produce 4" Mabob (2)
Move 3" Majig (2)					Produce 3" Mabob (2)
	MOVE ORDERING POST			PRODUCTION ORDERING POST	

◄···· Inbound ···· Processing ···· Outbound ····►

Layout for Workstation 3

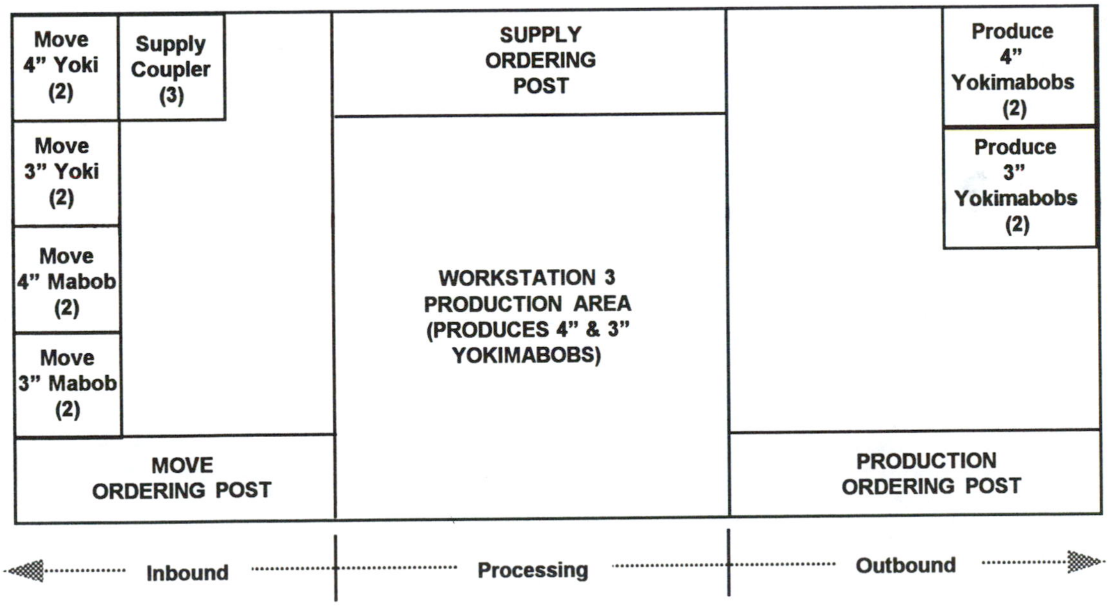

Move 4" Yoki (2)	Supply Coupler (3)	SUPPLY ORDERING POST		Produce 4" Yokimabobs (2)
Move 3" Yoki (2)				Produce 3" Yokimabobs (2)
Move 4" Mabob (2)		WORKSTATION 3 PRODUCTION AREA (PRODUCES 4" & 3" YOKIMABOBS)		
Move 3" Mabob (2)				
	MOVE ORDERING POST		PRODUCTION ORDERING POST	

◄···· Inbound ···· Processing ···· Outbound ····►

Numbers in parentheses indicate number of containers/kanban.

Yokimabobs

Production Kanbans

PRODUCE		

WHAT 3" Thinga
HOW MANY 5
PROCURE (for each)
   1) One 3/4" Bolt
   2) One Nut
 	
HOW   Screw Nut
tight onto Bolt
 	
2
	WHAT 4" Majig
	HOW MANY 5
	PROCURE (for each)
	   1) One 2 1/2"" Bolt
	   2) Three Nuts
	   3) Two Washers
	HOW Screw 2 Nuts
	tight onto Bolt; put on 2
	Washers; Screw 1 Nut
	tight against Washers.
	
	2
		WHAT 3" Majig
		HOW MANY 5
		PROCURE (for each)
		   1) One 2" Bolt
		   2) Two Nuts
		   3) One Washer
		HOW Screw 1 Nut
		tight onto Bolt. Put on
		Washer. Screw 1 Nut
		tight against Washer.
		
		2

PRODUCE	**PRODUCE**	**PRODUCE**

WHAT 4" Yoki
HOW MANY 5
PROCURE (for each)
   1) One Washer
   2) One 4" Thinga
   3) One Nut
HOW   Put Washer
onto 4" Thinga. Screw
Nut tight against Washer.
 	
2
	WHAT 3" Yoki
	HOW MANY 5
	PROCURE (for each)
	   1) One Washer
	   2) One Nut
	   3) One 3" Thinga
	HOW Put Washer
	onto 3" Thinga. Screw
	Nut tight against Washer.
	
	2
		WHAT 4" Mabob
		HOW MANY 5
		PROCURE (for each)
		   1) Three Nuts
		   2) Two Washers
		   3) One 4" Majig
		HOW Screw 1 Nut
		tight onto 4" Majig. Put on
		2 Washers. Screw 2 Nuts
		tight against Washers.
		
		2

PRODUCE	**PRODUCE**	**PRODUCE**

WHAT 3" Mabob
HOW MANY 5
PROCURE (for each)
   1) One Nut
   2) One Washer
   3) One 3" Majig
HOW
Put on 1 Washer. Screw
Nut tight against Washer.
 	
2
	WHAT 4" Yokimabob
	HOW MANY 5
	PROCURE (for each)
	   1) One Coupler
	   2) One 4" Yoki
	   3) One 4" Mabob
	HOW Screw one 4"
	Yoki tight into Coupler.
	Screw 4" Mabob tight
	into Coupler.
	
	2
		WHAT 3" Yokimabob
		HOW MANY 5
		PROCURE (for each)
		   1) One Coupler
		   2) One 3" Yoki
		   3) One 3" Mabob
		HOW Screw one 3"
		Yoki tight into Coupler.
		Screw 3" Mabob tight
		into Coupler.
		
		2

Yokimabobs
Move Kanbans

MOVE		
WHAT	4" Thinga	
HOW MANY	5	
FROM	Workstation 1 Outbound	
TO	Workstation 2 Inbound	
	2	

MOVE		
WHAT	3" Thinga	
HOW MANY	5	
FROM	Workstation 1 Outbound	
TO	Workstation 2 Inbound	
	2	

MOVE		
WHAT	4" Majig	
HOW MANY	5	
FROM	Workstation 1 Outbound	
TO	Workstation 2 Inbound	
	2	

MOVE		
WHAT	3" Majig	
HOW MANY	5	
FROM	Workstation 1 Outbound	
TO	Workstation 2 Inbound	
	2	

MOVE		
WHAT	4" Yoki	
HOW MANY	5	
TO	Workstation 2 Outbound	
	Workstation 3 Inbound	
	2	

MOVE		
WHAT	3" Yoki	
HOW MANY	5	
TO	Workstation 2 Outbound	
	Workstation 3 Inbound	
	2	

MOVE		
WHAT	4" Mabob	
HOW MANY	5	
FROM	Workstation 2 Outbound	
TO	Workstation 3 Inbound	
	2	

MOVE		
WHAT	3" Mabob	
HOW MANY	5	
FROM	Workstation 2 Outbound	
TO	Workstation 3 Inbound	
	2	

PRODUCE		
WHAT	4" Thinga	
HOW MANY	5	
PROCURE (for each)		
1) One 1" Bolt		
2) One Nut		
HOW	Screw Nut tight onto Bolt	
	2	

Yokimabobs

Supply Kanbans

SUPPLY		
WHAT		3/4" Bolt
HOW MANY		5
TO		Workstation 1 Inbound
		2

SUPPLY		
WHAT		1" Bolt
HOW MANY		5
TO		Workstation 1 Inbound
		2

SUPPLY		
WHAT		2" Bolt
HOW MANY		5
TO		Workstation 1 Inbound
		2

SUPPLY		
WHAT		2 1/2" Bolt
HOW MANY		5
TO		Workstation 1 Inbound
		2

SUPPLY		
WHAT		Nut
HOW MANY		5
TO		Workstation 1 Inbound
		4

SUPPLY		
WHAT		Washer
HOW MANY		5
TO		Workstation 1 Inbound
		3

SUPPLY		
WHAT		Nut
HOW MANY		5
TO		Workstation 2 Inbound
		4

SUPPLY		
WHAT		Washer
HOW MANY		5
TO		Workstation 2 Inbound
		3

SUPPLY		
WHAT		Coupler
HOW MANY		5
TO		Workstation 3 Inbound
		3

Inventory Counts Sheet

No.	Item	Initial Count	Count 1	Count 2	Count 3	Count 4	Count 5
1	4" Yokimabob	10					
2	3" Yokimabob	10					
3	4" Yoki	20					
4	3" Yoki	20					
5	4" Mabob	20					
6	3" Mabob	20					
7	4" Thinga	20					
8	3" Thinga	20					
9	4" Majig	20					
10	3" Majig	20					
11	2½" Bolt	10					
12	2" Bolt	10					
13	1" Bolt	10					
14	¾" Bolt	10					
15	Nut	40					
16	Washer	30					
17	Coupler	15					
	Total No.	305					
	% Decrease						
	Reason for Decrease						

PDCA

Topic   Yield, yield improvement

Purpose   To demonstrate the effect of yield changes on variable costs.

Materials   A roll of pennies
                   A calculator
                   PDCA worksheet

Players   Small groups

Introduction   Paper Diamond and Circles Associates (PDCA) is a secondary supplier to the parlor game industry. It produces two products that are used extensively as component parts for place markers, game boards, and spinners. The first is a 3/4 inch diameter paper circle. The second is a paper diamond with perimeter equal to four inches and a height of 1.414 inches. Each of the diamond's angles measures 90 degrees. Each product is made from first quality paper stock that has no grain or pattern.

The process for producing both products is identical. The raw material is fed into a press that cuts out the circles or diamonds from each piece of stock (an 8½ by 11 inch sheet of 20 pound bond paper for the diamonds, a 6.375 by 8.25 inch sheet of similar stock for the circles). The cutting device is similar to a big cookie cutter.

As currently configured, if paper circles are being cut, each piece of paper produces 88 units, if diamonds, 77 per sheet.

Paper can be purchased from the supplier in any size. Management has just received word from their paper supplier of another price increase. This makes three increases in the past six months and there is a concern about a severe paper shortage in the next year. The price of standard size (8½ by 11 inches) is $2 per sheet. The price of custom-cut stock is 2.4 cents per square inch. As the plant manager you have just been told that "Yield rates must improve!"

This exercise was created by Peter Arnold, Ph.D., Associate Professor of Operations Management, Boston University, Boston, Massachusetts.

Action Calculate the current yield on both paper circles and paper diamonds. (Hint: The area of a circle is equal to πr^2 and the area of a diamond is equal to ½pq (where p and q are the diagonals of the diamond and, in this case, are identical and equal to 1.414.) Figure 1 shows the die arrangement (reduced in size) for paper diamonds; Figure 2 shows the die arrangement (actual size) for paper circles.

Figure 1: Paper Diamond Die Arrangement

- How can the yield on paper diamond production be improved?

- How can the yield on paper circle production be improved? (The paper circles are exactly the size of pennies, which you can use to experiment with other die arrangements.)

- Evaluate the cost of each improvement option.

COMMON CAUSE
OR SPECIAL CAUSE?

Topic

Process Variation

Variation refers to the differences that can be observed or measured in outputs that are intended to be the same. With the appropriate measurement tools, that variation can be detected. In any production process it is important to distinguish between two important categories of variation: variation due to common causes and variation due to special causes. Common causes of variation are random and cannot be eliminated. In contrast, special causes of variation can be identified, analyzed, and remedied.

Purpose

The purpose of this exercise is to explore the nature of variation in processes and to consider the ways that variation can be managed.

Materials

Cardboard tube (such as a paper towel tube)
Several pennies
Marker pen
Three targets (Figure 1, or drawn on an overhead transparency)

Players

Three players per team

Player #1 is responsible for positioning the tube over the target and maintaining its position. Player #2 drops coins through the tube. Player #3 is responsible for marking where each coin first hits the target.

Action
Set-up

To simulate the set-up of an operation, Player #1 positions the tube approximately one foot above and directly over the center of the target and Player #2 drops a coin through the tube five times. Player #1 should adjust the position of the tube until the coins fall as close to the bull's-eye as possible. Make no marks on the target during set-ups.

This exercise was created by Donald G. Sluti, Ph.D., Assistant Professor of Production and Operations Management at the School of Business and Technology, University of Nebraska at Kearney.

First Pass: Once the set-up has been completed and the tube correctly positioned, Player #1 should tilt it slightly (about 20 degrees). Player #2 should drop five more coins through the tube and Player #3 should mark the position of each coin on the first target.

Second Pass: Player #1 tube should adjust the position of the tube to correct the tilt and the team should perform another set-up, making no marks on the target.

Once the set-up is complete, Player #2 should again drop five coins through the tube and Player #3 should mark where they fall on the second target.

Final Pass: Repeat the set-up steps.

Player #2 should drop a coin through the tube and Player #3 should mark the third target at the point where the coin lands. At this point, Player #1 should adjust the location of the tube by the distance the coin was from the center of the bull's-eye. This drop-mark-adjust sequence should be repeated five times.

Experimentation   What would happen if this process used different materials (different size coins)?

What would happen if the equipment was modified (longer or shorter tubes)?

Questions for Discussion   What were the causes of the variation for each pass?

What are the managerial implications of this experiment?

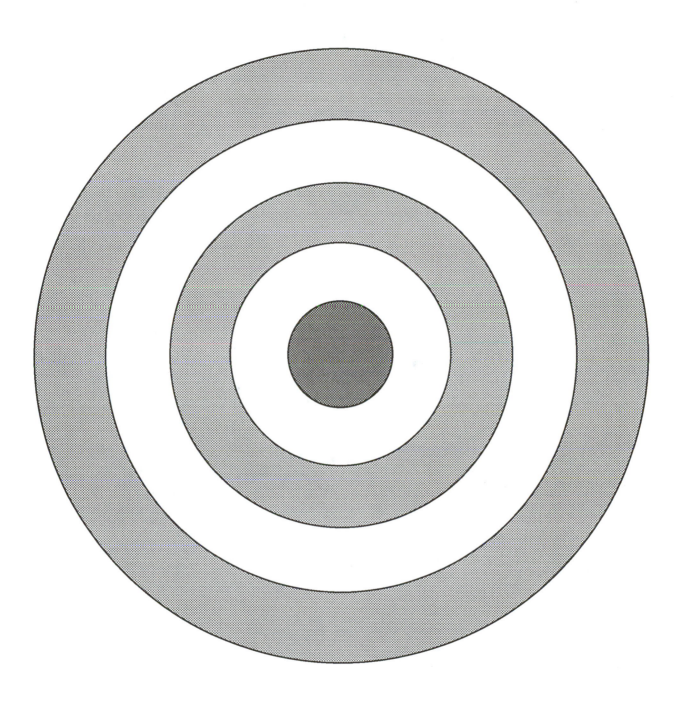

Quality Airplanes

Topic   Dimensions of Quality

Purpose   The purpose of this exercise is to introduce the concept of the multiple dimensions of quality and to apply those dimensions to a simple product.

Introduction   "Quality" is a complex construct that incorporates several important dimensions. Performance quality relates to the product's primary operating characteristics. It incorporates both product-defined characteristics and characteristics important to the customer. A product's features are secondary characteristics that supplement the product's basic function. Features are the "bells and whistles" that each customer can decide are important or unimportant. Reliability refers to the probability of a product's malfunctioning or failing within a specified period of time (the mean time to first failure, the mean time between failures, or the failure rate per unit of time). Customers are most concerned about reliability when they are purchasing durable goods and when downtime and maintenance are expensive. Durability is a measure of product life. In the technical sense, it can be measured as the amount a product is used before it physically deteriorates. When repair is possible, the customer evaluates durability as the trade-off between repair and replacement — which suggests that there is a close link between durability and reliability. Conformance quality is the degree to which a product's design and operating characteristics meet standards or specifications. This dimension of quality is measurable by the producer and can be monitored using statistical process control and sampling techniques. Serviceability refers to the speed, courtesy, competence and ease of repair of a product. Aesthetic quality is related to the appearance of the product or to other sensory characteristics (such as sounds or scents). Finally, perceived quality refers to the image of quality evoked by the product or its producer, brand image, for example. [See Garvin, David, *Managing Quality,* The Free Press, New York, 1988; and Garvin, David, "Competing on the Eight Dimensions of Quality," *Harvard Business Review*, November - December 1987.]

This exercise was created by Janelle Heineke, DBA, Assistant Professor of Operations Management, Boston University, Boston, Massachusetts.

This exercise applies the dimensions of quality to a simple product: paper airplanes.

Materials

A stack of plain white typing paper
One ruler
One tape measure
Colored markers

Players

Aerodynamic Design Engineer teams: groups of 3
Inspector team: group of 3
Customer team: group of 3

Action

Phase 1:

In 10-15 minutes, each team will accomplish the following assignments:

Design Team

The Design Team will design and produce a prototype airplane.

Inspector Team

The Inspector Team will develop a plan to evaluate the planes produced by each Design Team.

Customer Team

The Customer Team will define its criteria for airplane purchase.

Phase 2:

Each Design Team will demonstrate the production of a single plane while a team spokesperson describes its product to the Customer Team. The Inspector Team will time the production task time (start to finish for the single unit) and define for the class the quality criteria it identified and the measurement scale it will use. The Inspector Team will then apply the quality evaluation criteria it developed to each plane. After quality inspection has been completed, the customer group will caucus briefly and will choose a model to purchase, explaining to the whole group why they made that choice.

Questions for Discussion

1. How were decisions about quality dimensions made within your groups? Why?

2. How could you change the design process to make it more efficient and effective?

Quality is Not Optional

Topic	Machine Capability Analysis (SPC)
Purpose	This exercise demonstrates the fundamentals of a machine capability study.
Introduction	A machine capability analysis is an important step in the use of Statistical Process Control. It compares the inherent variation of a process, determined through data collection when the process is in control*, and the customer's specifications. If the output of the process falls consistently within the customer's specifications, the customer will be satisfied with the output and the process is considered to be capable. If, however, the output of the process does not consistently fall within the customer's specifications, the process is considered to be incapable.
Materials	A pencil or pen A standard pair of dice for each player Quality Worksheet
Players	At least six players Each player is a worker at Precision Bearings, a company famed for its high precision and outgoing quality and for its extensive training of new employees. One General Manager, played by the instructor.
Action Overview	On this job, workers operate identical machines (the dice) to bore and hone an outer bearing race (see Figure 1), which must, when complete, measure 1.6207" inside diameter, ±0.0003". The number rolled on the dice indicates how many ten-thousandths of an inch the inner diameter measures above 1.6200". The target value is seven, but any outcome between four and ten is an acceptable product.

> * A process is in control when it is behaving normally; that is, any variation present is due to random causes.

This exercise was created by Duncan C. McDougall, DBA, Associate Professor of Operations Management at Plymouth State College, Plymouth, New Hampshire.

A unit is produced each time the dice are rolled. Record each roll on the Quality Worksheet.

Pass 1

Make 10 bearing races and record their inner diameters on the Quality Worksheet. Count all defective units (2, 3, 11, or 12) and calculate the percentage defective (since there were ten units produced, this will be the number of defectives times 10).

Stop production, and indicate that you are through by turning your Quality Worksheet toward the front of the table, and placing your pencil on it. At this time, the General Manager will review your work.

Pass 2

Make 10 more bearing races and record their inner diameters on the Quality Worksheet. Again, count defective units and calculate the percentage defective.

Again, the General Manager will pause production to evaluate worker performance.

Capability
Study and

A form will be distributed showing the results of the capability study on your equipment.

Process Improvement

What is the expected defect rate in this process?
Whose fault are those defects?
Who's taking the blame?
What must be done to prevent defects?

Pass 3

Based on the machine capability study, modifications will be made to reduce the inherent variation in the machines used at Precision Bearing. Each machine consists of only one die and the die reading represents the number of ten-thousands above 1.62035". The target value is 3.5 ± 3.

Using the new improved process described by the General Manager, you will produce an additional ten bearing races and record their inside diameters on the Quality Worksheet.

**Questions for
Discussion**

1. What are the work floor implications of having a capability study done on each process before releasing it to production?

2. What benefits might accrue to the management and owners from such a practice?

3. What would it be like to work in a plant where the variability inherent in production processes had not been quantified?

Quality is Not Optional

Quality Worksheet

Record Inner Diameter as ± ten thousandths of target value			
Unit	Pass 1	Pass 2	Pass 3
1			
2			
3			
4			
5			
6			
7			
8			
9			
10			
# Defective			
% Defective			

Out of Control

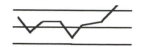

Topic   Attribute statistical process control (SPC)

Purpose   This exercise demonstrates the fundamentals of attribute SPC using *p* charts: calculating control limits, drawing samples, charting sample means, and interpreting an SPC chart.

Introduction   SPC was introduced by Walter Shewhart, a statistician at Bell Laboratories, who discovered in the 1930s that random variation is present in all processes. Once the usual random variation for a process has been studied and quantified, a worker can monitor the process in real time and, using control charts and basic statistics, determine whether the degree of variation is still random or whether some new "special" cause of variation has been introduced. SPC can be used with attribute data, which is counted (good or bad, non-defective or defective, present or absent, etc.) or with variable data, which is measured (length, width, specific gravity, tensile strength, etc.).

For either attribute or variable data, SPC begins with observing the underlying variation in a process. First, a large data set is collected when the process is believed to be operating as it should be. This is important because an SPC chart should be constructed when only the process's inherent random variation is present. Next, the process mean and standard deviation are calculated. The mean of the data set will be the center line in the control chart; the standard deviations will be used to calculate "control limits." SPC is based on a fundamental statistical rule, the Central Limit Theorem, which assures us that, whatever the shape of the underlying distribution, the means of samples of a given size drawn from that distribution will be normally distributed. The Central Limit Theorem allows us to apply what we know about normal distributions to the distribution of the means of samples drawn from any production process.

This exercise was created by Janelle Heineke, DBA, Assistant Professor of Operations Management, Boston University and Larry Meile, Ph.D, Assistant Professor of Operations Management, Whittemore School of Business, University of New Hampshire, Durham, New Hampshire.

This exercise focuses on the p-chart, which is used when the underlying percentage of an attribute is being monitored (such as the percent defective in a production process). Once we know, from our initial data analysis, the long-run percent (p) of the attribute we are observing, we can use p and the size of the samples drawn (n) to calculate the standard deviation of the sample distribution:

$$\sqrt{\frac{p(1-p)}{n}}$$

It should be clear from this formula that two factors affect the size of the standard deviation: p and n. What happens to the standard deviation when either increases? When either decreases?

Remember, the standard deviation is a measure of a distribution's dispersion or spread. A tall, thin distribution has a small standard deviation; a short, fat distribution has a larger standard deviation.

In a normal distribution, approximately 68% of the distribution lies between ± 1 standard deviation from the mean, approximately 95% lies between ± 2 standard deviations from the mean, and approximately 99.7% lies between ± 3 standard deviations from the mean. We should be able to expect, then, that when a process is varying in its usual random way nearly all of the distribution will fall between ± 3 standard deviations. Because this is true, the control limits are usually set at three standard deviations. If a sample mean falls outside the three standard deviation control limits it is very likely (99.7%) that the system is not behaving in its usual random way.

Once the mean and standard deviation of the process have been calculated a control chart can be constructed with p as the center line and the control limits set at ± 3 standard deviations:

UCL

Center Line

LCL

A system is in control when it behaves as it is expected to behave, given the calculated mean and standard deviation of the process. By plotting the percent of the attribute in the sample on a control chart, non-random patterns can be identified as they happen, permitting the worker to stop the process and look for the cause of non-random variation.

Because the standard deviation calculation depends on the size of the sample, deciding on the appropriate size for a sample is also important. When doing attribute SPC, the sample should be large enough to find at least one (and preferably two) defects for the given p, on average. What size should the sample be, then, if the value of p is .1? [To see, on average, two defects per sample, the sample size would need to be 20: $.1 (n) = 2$; $n = 2/.1 = 20$]

The following exercise allows you to see the effects of changing the sample size and the percent of an attribute in the population being monitored (in this case, the percent of defective units).

Materials

A deck of playing cards, with one black and one red ace removed. [This leaves fifty cards, making percentage calculations easier.]

Control Chart worksheets.

Players

Two production workers:
    Worker #1 samples
    Worker #2 charts sample means

Action

Workers #1 and #2 calculate the 3-standard deviation control limits for each pass. Worker #1 should thoroughly shuffle the deck and draw a sample of the appropriate size (n). For each sample, Worker #2 calculates the percentage defective in the sample (number of defectives x two), charts the sample percent defective on the chart, and returns the sample to the deck. The shuffle, sample, calculate procedure is repeated for each sample.

Pass 1:
$p = .2$; $n = 10$

Calculate control limits and label Chart 1.
Twos, threes, and aces are defectives. since 10 of the 50 cards are "defects", the proportion of defectives is: $10/50 = 20\%$, therefore $p = .2$. Draw ten samples of size 10 and chart.

Pass 2: $p = .2$; $n = 20$	Calculate new control limits and label Chart 2. How do the control limits differ from those calculated in Pass 1? Draw ten samples of size 20 and chart.
Pass 3: $p = .1$; $n = 20$	Calculate new control limits and label Chart 3. How do the control limits differ from those calculated in Passes 1 & 2? Twos and the black ace are defectives. Draw ten samples of size 20 and chart.
Pass 4: Out of Control	Use the same chart as Pass 3. The process has changed since Pass 3 and is now producing more defectives (twos, threes and both aces are defectives). Draw 10 samples (do not change sample size) and chart. What has happened to the pattern you observed in Pass 3? Does the pattern look random?

Questions for Discussion

1. What happened to the control limits when sample size increased for a given p?

2. What happened to control limits when p increased?

3. What happened to the control chart when the process started producing more defects?

4. Why should sample sizes for attribute SPC be based on the long-run p?

5. When collecting the initial data to calculate control limits, how can you be sure the process is operating with only random variation (in control)?

6. Identify some manufacturing or service situations where it might be useful to implement an attribute SPC system.

7. If you were the supervisor of a production process that used SPC charts, what rules of thumb might you develop to help workers identify when a process is out of control?

8. When a process has been determined to be out of control, what should the worker do? Why?

9. What are the two types of errors that can be made in interpreting control charts? What would happen to the risks of those errors if the control limits were set at ± 2 standard deviations from the mean? at ± 6 standard deviations from the mean?

10. It is often remarked in introductory SPC classes that SPC might be useful for manufacturing but is probably not applicable to service operations. What do you think?

Control Chart Worksheets

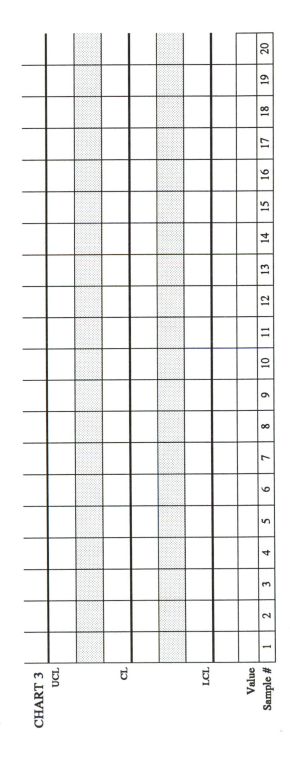

CHART 1

UCL										
CL										
LCL										
Value										
Sample #	1	2	3	4	5	6	7	8	9	10

CHART 2

UCL										
CL										
LCL										
Value										
Sample #	1	2	3	4	5	6	7	8	9	10

CHART 3

UCL																				
CL																				
LCL																				
Value																				
Sample #	1	2	3	4	5	6	7	8	9	10	11	12	13	14	15	16	17	18	19	20

Domini Sugar Company

Topic   Variables Statistical Process Control

Purpose   This exercise introduces the student to Statistical Process Control (SPC). Participants will develop an X-bar chart and range chart for a sugar packaging operation.

Introduction Ms. Susan Sugarbaker is an operations manager for the Domini Sugar Company. The Company has just installed a new filling machine (the Whalabrader M106 Filler) which is to be used to fill 1 lb. boxes of table sugar for the grocery market.

After the initial installation of the M106 Filler, trial runs proved to be disappointing. The major problem was product starvation of one or more of the two nozzles because the sugar wouldn't automatically flow downward from the feed hopper. This is a common problem when dry granulated material is to be fed to a nozzle system. The problem was so severe that over 30% of the boxes of sugar were under the stated weight by two or more ounces.

The Domini Sugar Company has a standing policy that the average weight of products shipped must be at or above the stated weight of the package label, so Susan certainly could not allow the packaging line to continue operation until corrections were made.

The process maintenance crew solved the sugar feeding problem by installing a compressed-air driven "thumper" on the feed hopper. The thumper vibrated the sheet metal hopper continuously which caused the sugar to flow evenly to the two nozzles. This approach eliminated the need to manually "thump" the hopper with a rubber hammer as had been done during the trial runs. The maintenance crew adjusted the air pressure and volume to get an effective vibration while attempting to minimize the noise level.

This exercise was created by William R. Benoit, Ph.D., Associate Professor of Operations Management and Duncan C. McDougall, Associate Professor of Operations Management, Plymouth State College, Plymouth, New Hampshire.

Nevertheless, the final noise level was high enough to require that filling-line workers wear hearing protection. Susan notified the company health nurse and arranged for periodic hearing examinations for each worker on the line. All supervisors were briefed on the procedures for ear protection and on the need to stop the packaging line in the event of a thumper or air supply failure.

After these modifications and procedures were in place, the packaging crew made a new trial run to "shake down" this new packaging line and to generate basic data for the development of initial X-bar and Range quality control charts. Susan decided to process sixty 1-lb. boxes of sugar on the new packaging line during the last few minutes of the work day, and planned to do the data analysis that evening. If the process proved to be set up properly, and in statistical control, Susan planned to stop the old packaging line the next day, and switch to the new line.

Susan headed home for dinner and looked forward to an evening of data analysis. She decided to call you to have dinner with her and expects your help with this analysis.

Materials SPC Worksheets
Calculators

Players Groups of two or three, all may participate

Action The raw data for the sixty-box trial run is listed below in TABLE I. Using the data in the table, develop the X-bar and R charts for the packaging line. The factors and formulae for the charts are contained in TABLE II.

The instructor will assign each group to construct its SPC charts using particular sample sizes: $n = 2, 3, 4, 5, 6, 10, 12,$ or 15.

Group the data into samples in sample number order (for example, if $n = 3$, the first sample has three weight measurements: 16.0, 15.9, and 16.0) Compute the mean and the range for each sample. Record the mean and range on the SPC Worksheet and plot the sample points on the graphs.

TABLE I: RAW DATA - WEIGHTS - SUGAR BOXES - 60 OBSERVATIONS

Box	Weight	Box	Weight	Box	Weight	Box	Weight
1	16.0	16	16.0	31	16.1	46	16.2
2	15.9	17	16.0	32	16.1	47	16.1
3	16.0	18	15.9	33	16.1	48	15.9
4	16.0	19	15.9	34	16.1	49	16.1
5	16.0	20	15.9	35	16.0	50	16.3
6	16.0	21	16.2	36	16.0	51	16.1
7	15.8	22	16.0	37	15.9	52	16.0
8	15.9	23	15.9	38	16.1	53	16.4
9	16.1	24	16.1	39	15.7	54	16.3
10	15.8	25	16.1	40	16.3	55	15.8
11	15.9	26	16.1	41	16.1	56	16.0
12	15.8	27	16.4	42	15.9	57	16.1
13	15.8	28	15.8	43	15.6	58	16.3
14	15.9	29	15.9	44	15.8	59	16.0
15	16.0	30	15.7	45	15.8	60	16.0

Questions for Discussion

1. Does the packaging line appear to be in statistical control? What is the effect of sample size on this assessment? Why?

2. Why is it important to use both average and range charts when doing SPC with continuous data?

3. Is the process producing package weights in compliance with the management directive?

4. What issues should Susan and Domini Sugar Company consider in making this switch to the new packaging line?

TABLE II: Factors for Computing Control Chart Limits

Sample Size n	Mean Factor A_2	Upper Range D_4	Lower Range D_3
2	1.880	3.268	0
3	0.023	2.574	0
4	0.729	2.282	0
5	0.577	2.114	0
6	0.483	2.004	0
7	0.419	1.924	0.076
8	0.373	1.864	0.136
9	0.337	1.816	0.184
10	0.308	1.777	0.223
12	0.266	1.716	0.284
14	0.235	1.671	0.329
16	0.212	1.636	0.364
18	0.194	1.608	0.392
20	0.180	1.586	0.414
25	0.153	1.541	0.459

Source: Render & Stair, *Quantitative Analysis for Management*, Edition 5, p. 233.

Formulae for X-bar/R Charts:

X-bar Chart Limits

$$UCL_{\bar{x}} = \bar{\bar{X}} + A_2 * \bar{R}$$

$$LCL_{\bar{x}} = \bar{\bar{X}} - A_2 * \bar{R}$$

R Chart Limits

$$UCL_R = D_4 * \bar{R}$$

$$LCL_R = D_3 * \bar{R}$$

Domini Sugar Company

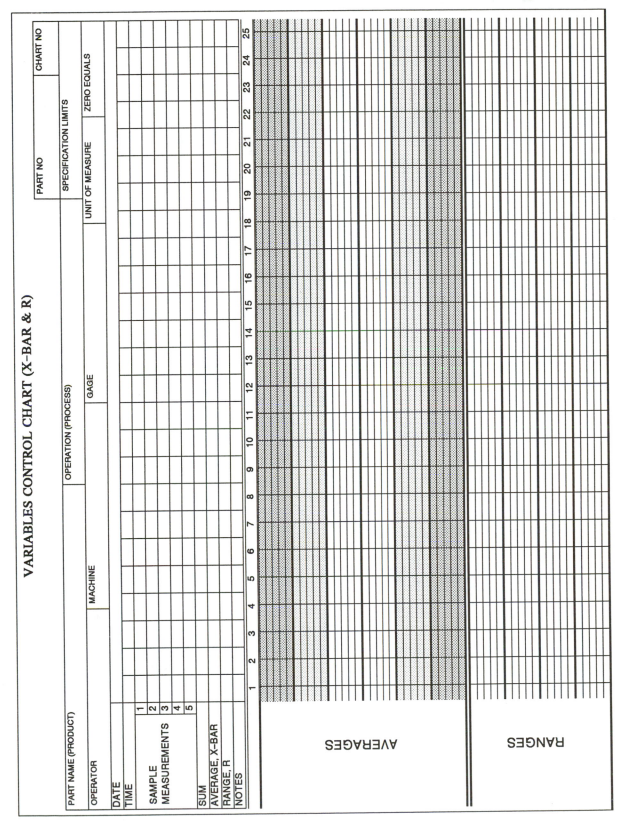

VARIABLES CONTROL CHART (X-BAR & R)

PART NAME (PRODUCT)

OPERATION (PROCESS)

PART NO

CHART NO

OPERATOR

MACHINE

GAGE

SPECIFICATION LIMITS

UNIT OF MEASURE

ZERO EQUALS

DATE

TIME

SAMPLE MEASUREMENTS

1
2
3
4
5

SUM

AVERAGE, X-BAR

RANGE, R

NOTES

AVERAGES

RANGES

211

Taguchi Airplanes

Topic   Experimental Design

Purpose   To demonstrate a Taguchi fractional factorial experiment.

Introduction   Genichi Taguchi is known for his contributions to both quality philosophy and quality tools. He maintains that effective quality control requires methods that focus on *making quality* rather than *inspecting quality in*, and proposes a three step approach: system design, parameter design, and tolerance design. *System design* produces the prototype product, considering both the needs of the customer and the capabilities of the manufacturing environment. *Parameter design* identifies the settings for product or process factors that improve the quality characteristic(s) and minimize the sensitivity of the design to sources of random variation. *Tolerance design* sets the tolerances around the target value, considering both the loss to the customer due to performance variation and the increase in manufacturing cost associated with reducing the deviation from the target value.

Taguchi's contributions to the tools of quality management and experimental design are related primarily to parameter design. He developed methods to shorten product development time and to improve quality based on financial cost/benefit analysis. His process for quality improvement and cost reduction is simple and straight-forward and his development of graphical ways for designing experiments has led to a resurgence of interest in the design of experiments.

This exercise provides an opportunity to perform an experiment testing the effects of four factors, each with three levels, on the flight distance of paper airplanes. If all combinations of factors and levels were tested, $3^4 = 81$ experiments would need to be performed. Replicating these experiments five times to understand variations would then require 81 x 5 = 405 trials. The effects of each factor

---

This exercise was created by Steven Eppinger, Ph.D., Associate Professor of Management Science, Massachusetts Institute of Technology Sloan School of Management, Cambridge, MA.

can be determined by using a carefully defined subset of experiments, called an **orthogonol** array.

Determining whether the level of a factor really affects the quality characteristic (in this case flight distance) requires more than intuition. A product's functional characteristics can be affected by two categories of factors: controllable factors (inputs) and uncontrollable factors (noise factors). Taguchi blends measures of the mean and variability of performance by analyzing the **signal-to-noise (S/N)** ratio. In its simplest form, the S/N ratio is the ratio of the mean to the standard deviation. Generally, maximizing the S/N ratio achieves robust product design.

The goal of this experiment is to design an airplane which flies far and can be folded and thrown by anyone. We will consider four factors: position of the weight, stabilizer folds, nose distance, and wing angle.

Materials

Taguchi Airplane Template
Paper clips (standard size)
Masking tape
Tape measure
Flight Distance Record
Design Analysis Tables

Players

Any number; all may participate:
  1 Recorder, who measures and records airplane flight distance
  All other participants test paper airplane flight. Each is assigned an experiment number by the instructor.

Action
Set-up

At one end of a hallway or long room (at least 30 feet), place a strip of masking tape on the floor to designate the launching station. Perpendicluar to this, lay a 30-foot strip of tape on the floor, numbered in one foot increments starting at the launch line, as shown in Figure 1.

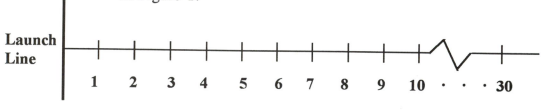

Launch Line

1 2 3 4 5 6 7 8 9 10 · · · 30

Figure 1

Each participant should take one paper clip and one Taguchi Airplane Template. Write the experiment number in the space provided and circle the appropriate level of each of the four parameters corresponding to the assigned experiment.

With print side face down, fold the template in half along the center line, then open it back up. Make four folds to create the tip, then re-fold along the center fold. Make wing and stabilizer folds along the appropriate lines for your assigned experiment, attempting to get the bends close to 90 degrees (See Figure 2).

Apply a paper clip weight in the correct location for your assigned experiment.

Stand at the launching station and throw the plane. For each of the nine experiments, nine paper airplanes should be folded.

The recorder should measure the distance flown; the Recorder should record the results of each trial in the Flight Distance Record. (Alternatively, participants can measure and record their own flight distances.)

In groups, complete the Design Analysis Tables.

Questions for Discussion

1. What can you say about the effects of the different factors on flight distance? What levels of each factor would you use to maximize flight distance?

2. What can you say about the effects of the different factors on variation in flight distance? What levels of each factor would you use to minimize variation in flight distance?

3. Is the S/N ratio a reasonable way to capture both goals (to maximize distance and minimize variation)? Can you specify an optimal design? Why or why not?

4. What types of noise (variations) are considered in this experiment?

5. How can interactions between factors be considered?

215

**Suggestions for
Additional Reading**

Box, G. and Bisgaard, S., "Statistical Tools for Improved Designs," *Mechanical Engineering*, January 1988, p. 32-40.

Byrne, D.M. and Taguchi, S., "The Taguchi Approach to Parameter Design," *Quality Progress*, December 1989.

Phadke, M.S., *Quality Engineering Using Robust Design*, Prentice Hall, Englewood Cliffs, NJ, 1989.

Ross, P.J., *Taguchi Techniques for Quality Engineering: Loss Function, Orthogonol Experiments, Parameter and Tolerance Design*, McGraw-Hill Book Company, New York, NY, 1988.

Taguchi, G. and Clausing, D., "Robust Quality," *Harvard Business Review*, January-February 1990.

Figure 2: Taguchi Airplane Folds

Fold 1: With print side face-down,
fold center fold, then open.

Fold 2

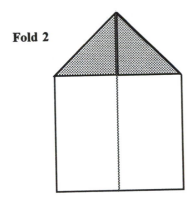

Fold 3

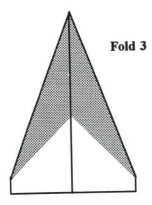

Folds 2 and 3 form tip of airplane.

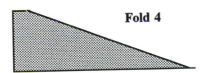

Fold 4

Refold center fold (Fold 4),
printed side out.

Fold 5

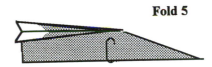

Make wing folds (Fold 5).
Attach paper clip in appropriate
place for assigned experiment.

Fold 6

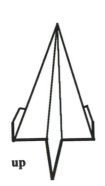

up   flat   down

Make stabilizer folds for assigned experiment (Fold 6).

TAGUCHI AIRPLANES FLIGHT DISTANCE RECORD

Experiment #	Repetition									Mean Distance	Standard Deviation	S/N
	1	2	3	4	5	6	7	8	9			
1												
2												
3												
4												
5												
6												
7												
8												
9												

Note: $S/N = 10 \ log \ [\frac{\overline{x}}{s}]^2$

219

TAGUCHI AIRPLANES DESIGN ANALYSIS TABLES

Experiment #	Design Parameter				Mean Distance	Standard Deviation	S/N Ratio
	Weight Location	Stabilizer Setting	Nose Length	Wing Angle			
1	A1	B1	C1	D1			
2	A1	B2	C2	D2			
3	A1	B3	C3	D3			
4	A2	B1	C2	D3			
5	A2	B2	C3	D1			
6	A2	B3	C1	D2			
7	A3	B1	C3	D2			
8	A3	B2	C1	D3			
9	A3	B3	C2	D1			

These three columns are
completed using the data
from the Distance Record

	Level	Design Parameter				
		A	B	C	D	
		Weight Location	Stabilizer Setting	Nose Length	Wing Angle	
Distance Means	Level 1					Use to find which parameter
	Level 2					setting gives greatest mean
	Level 3					flying distance.
Standard Deviation Means	Level 1					Use to find which parameter
	Level 2					setting is most robust to
	Level 3					noise.
S/N Ratios Means	Level 1					Use to find which parameter
	Level 2					setting represents a reasonable
	Level 3					trade-off.

Use the values in the table above to complete this table. For example,
Experiments 1, 2, and 3 have Factor A (Weight Location) at level 1, so use
the means, standard deviations, and S/N ratios from those three experiments to
calculate the level one settings for Factor A.

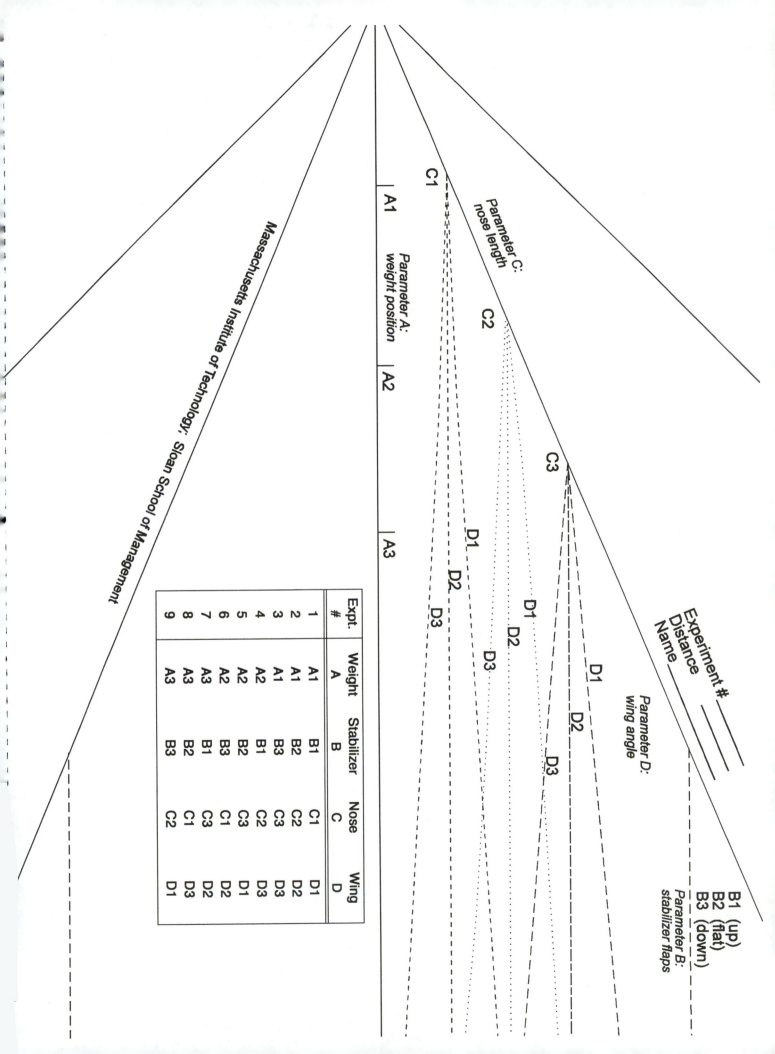

Experiment #
Distance
Name

Parameter A: weight position — A1, A2, A3

Parameter B: stabilizer flaps — B1 (up), B2 (flat), B3 (down)

Parameter C: nose length — C1, C2, C3

Parameter D: wing angle — D1, D2, D3

Expt. #	Weight A	Stabilizer B	Nose C	Wing D
1	A1	B1	C1	D1
2	A1	B2	C2	D2
3	A1	B3	C3	D3
4	A2	B1	C2	D3
5	A2	B2	C3	D1
6	A2	B3	C1	D2
7	A3	B1	C3	D2
8	A3	B2	C1	D3
9	A3	B3	C2	D1

Massachusetts Institute of Technology; Sloan School of Management

Catapulting Coins

Topic   Experimental design, robust process design

Purpose   This exercise gives an opportunity to think about the design of an experiment which investigates how various factors influence an outcome. The task is to measure the height to which a coin is launched by a ruler catapult under varying conditions.

Introduction   Process variation is caused by changes in the controllable and uncontrollable variables that affect performance. The settings of some process variables are very critical. Small changes in these values can cause significant changes in the output. Other variables can vary over a reasonably broad range and not change the outcome very much. Furthermore there may be ranges of values for these variables where the system is less sensitive to change than in other ranges. Since uncontrollable variations (random effects or common cause) will always occur, designing processes to run in the insensitive range will minimize the random variation in the output. Operating processes where the system is least sensitive to change is one key concept of robust process design.

Materials
1 ruler
1 pencil or marker pen
2 coins (quarters are suggested)
1 yard stick
1 Data Collection Worksheet
2 Data Graphing Worksheets

Players   Divide into groups of two or three.
> One player will adjust the catapult and launch the coin
> One player will report the maximum height for each trial
> One player will record the results

If teams of two are formed, the observation and recording tasks can be combined.

This exercise was created by Larry Meile, Professor of Operations Management at the Whittemore School of Business and Economics, University of New Hampshire, Durham, NH.

Games and Exercises for Operations Management

Action

Experiment to find the effect of varying the distance from the anchored end to the fulcrum (distance A) and the mode of release by launching and recording ten shots for each combination on the worksheet. To launch the quarter, have the catapult operator hold one end of the ruler firmly on the table top while moving the pencil to the desired position. The quarter is then placed on the ruler, centered over the 11-inch mark. Press the free end of the ruler down, bending it until the end touches the table top. Let the end snap up, catapulting the quarter into the air.

The catapult operator will be launching the quarter two ways. The first method is to depress and release the ruler with his or her finger. The second is to depress the ruler with a coin held near to horizontal (another quarter works nicely) which is then slipped off the end of the ruler to launch the coin.

The performance criterion is the height the coin reaches on each flight. To effectively measure the height of the flight the observer should stand back and estimate the top of the coin's flight as measured by a vertical yard stick. So that the observer can readjust his or her gaze, fire a shot or two before starting to record data for a new position.

For each of the experimental combinations on the worksheet, find the mean height of the ten trials and calculate its standard deviation. Then plot the results on the graph.

Questions for Discussion

1) Describe the factors which you think influenced the outcome.

2) Which of these are under your control? Which are not?

3) Which methods and what settings produced the best results?

4) How should "best" be defined?

5) If you were interested in running this process so that the output would be most consistent, what position would you choose for the fulcrum and what releasing method would be preferred?

Figure 1. Pencil and Ruler Catapult

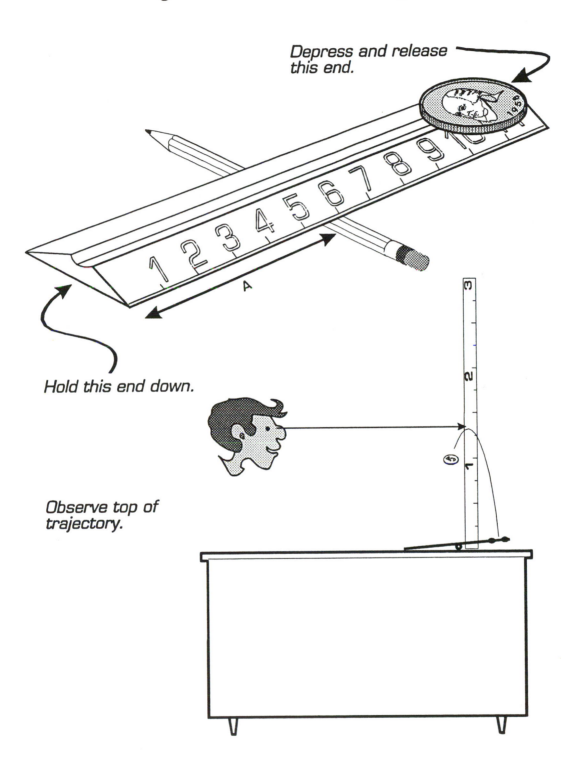

Depress and release this end.

Hold this end down.

Observe top of trajectory.

CATAPULTING COINS
DATA COLLECTION WORKSHEET

Fulcrum at:

TRIAL

	1	2	3	4	5	6	7	8	9	10	Average	Std. Dev.
F R I N G E R S E 3"												
4"												
5"												
6"												
7"												
8"												
9"												

	1	2	3	4	5	6	7	8	9	10	Average	Std. Dev.
C O I N A S E 3"												
4"												
5"												
6"												
7"												
8"												
9"												

229

CATAPULTING COINS
DATA GRAPHING WORKSHEET

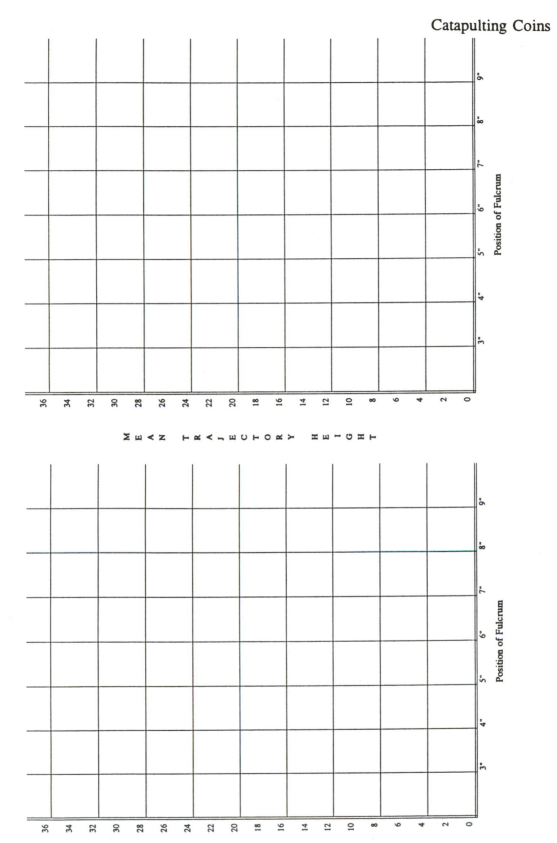